Praise for
Stay Home, Stay Happy

"Rachel's breezy style combined with a compelling story helps this inspirational parenting book rise above the others. She's hip, she's smart, and her 'no apologies' approach to stay-at-home parenting will help other moms feel not meek but mighty."

—Juliet Huddy, *The Morning Show with Mike and Juliet*

"More profound than a basic self-help book. *Stay Home, Stay Happy* isn't just about making the house run better or making one's self feel better. It gets to the essence of finding fulfillment and happiness with the choices we make."

—Pia de Solenni, SThD, MoralTheologian.com

STAY HOME, STAY HAPPY

10 Secrets to Loving

At-Home Motherhood

RACHEL CAMPOS-DUFFY

A CELEBRA BOOK

Celebra
Published by New American Library, a division of
Penguin Group (USA) Inc., 375 Hudson Street, New York, New York 10014, USA
Penguin Group (Canada), 90 Eglinton Avenue East, Suite 700, Toronto, Ontario
M4P 2Y3, Canada (a division of Pearson Penguin Canada Inc.)
Penguin Books Ltd., 80 Strand, London WC2R 0RL, England
Penguin Ireland, 25 St. Stephen's Green, Dublin 2, Ireland
(a division of Penguin Books Ltd.)
Penguin Group (Australia), 250 Camberwell Road, Camberwell, Victoria 3124,
Australia (a division of Pearson Australia Group Pty. Ltd.)
Penguin Books India Pvt. Ltd., 11 Community Centre, Panchsheel Park,
New Delhi - 110 017, India
Penguin Group (NZ), 67 Apollo Drive, Rosedale, North Shore 0632,
New Zealand (a division of Pearson New Zealand Ltd.)
Penguin Books (South Africa) (Pty.) Ltd., 24 Sturdee Avenue, Rosebank,
Johannesburg 2196, South Africa

Penguin Books Ltd., Registered Offices: 80 Strand, London WC2R 0RL, England

First published by Celebra, a division of Penguin Group (USA) Inc.

First Printing, September 2009
10   9   8   7   6   5   4   3   2   1

Copyright © Rachel Campos-Duffy, 2009
All rights reserved

CELEBRA and logo are trademarks of Penguin Group (USA) Inc.

LIBRARY OF CONGRESS CATALOGING-IN-PUBLICATION DATA:

Campos-Duffy, Rachel.
Stay home, stay happy: 10 secrets to loving at-home motherhood/
Rachel Campos-Duffy.
        p. cm.
Includes bibliographical references and index.
    ISBN 978-0-451-22807-9
    1. Motherhood.   2. Mothers.   3. Mothers—Family relationships.
    4. Housewives.   I. Title.
    HQ759.C262 2009
    646.70085'2—dc22   2009016984

Set in Minion
Designed by Jessica Shatan Heslin/Studio Shatan, Inc.

Printed in the United States of America

PUBLISHER'S NOTE
While the author has made every effort to provide accurate telephone numbers and Internet
addresses at the time of publication, neither the publisher nor the author assumes any
responsibility for errors, or for changes that occur after publication. Further, publisher does
not have any control over and does not assume any responsibility for author or third-party
Web sites or their content.

Evita, Jack, Lucia-Belen, John-Paul and Paloma
You've made it more fun than I could have ever imagined.

Sean
Ten years and I still can't believe my luck.

Ruth
The wisdom you imparted shall ever remain.

ACKNOWLEDGMENTS

Julie, my sister, my friend, without you I could have never launched or completed this project. We are a good team.

Cat, thank you for still believing in me after all these years. I cherish our friendship.

Maura, my literary agent, you are simply the best.

Tracy, my editor, I have learned so much from you. Thank you for your patience.

Ray, thank you for your enthusiasm and continued belief in this project.

Mama and Pappi, thank you for loving me and always valuing my life as an at-home mom.

Leah, your friendship means the world to me.

Frank Folino, thank you for loving our family.

Tía Nieves, thank you for your love.

To all the mothers who have mentored me.

And most especially to God and our Blessed Mother, who have always held me in their tender care.

CONTENTS

STAY HOME,
STAY HAPPY

INTRODUCTION

Soon after my latest child was born, on a beautiful Wisconsin spring morning, I packed up the kids for a trip to the park. My husband was out of town on business and this was my first excursion alone with all five children. Though by any standard I would be considered an "experienced" mom, truthfully, I was a little nervous. I wondered if I would be able to handle them by myself. My body hadn't quite recovered from Paloma's birth, and my energy and reflexes were sluggish from late-night feedings. Nonetheless, in Wisconsin good weather is fleeting, and I knew my kids would appreciate playing with all the other winter-weary children at the local park. And so we all piled into the car.

Immediately after the car stopped, the kids popped the car door open and spilled out of the minivan into the park, running in every which direction. I watched the ensuing chaos from a bench, holding the baby, and felt my trepidation slip away. Eventually, my sweet and pensive six-year-old son, Jack, took a break from the action and wandered over to me and the baby. Playing with his two-week-old sister's feet, he exclaimed, "Oh, Mommy! She's soooo cuuute. . . . I didn't know your belly could work so well." My heart melted. I filed the moment away in my mind, where I store all the precious things my kids say (instead of the far more reliable practice of dutifully writing them down for easy wedding-day retrieval). Kids often say things unexpectedly profound, and I grasped a profound truth in Jack's gentle words: *I didn't know my belly would work so well either.* Or that becoming a mom would so completely transform me and, in the process, my definition of happiness and success. I often think back to the day that unexpectedly changed my life, my attitude, and the way that I saw myself as an at-home mom.

That morning in 2003, the phone finally rang. I knew it was Barbara Walters—Barbara Walters and Bill Geddie, the executive producers of *The View.* I had spent several weeks guest cohosting on the show, and was a finalist for the open cohost spot. Now Barbara and Bill were calling the three finalists to inform them who had been selected to fill that vacant seat. Anxiety, excitement, and even a dose of confidence were fighting for space inside my stomach. My entire midsection was a tightly wound knot bound together with so many different emotions.

This call had the potential to instantly transform my career from fading reality TV personality to bona fide daytime TV star. A Hispanic woman had never before been given such a platform on daytime television. A part of me was confident that the nationwide hunt to fill *The View*'s open slot would end in this groundbreaking result. But I focused too on another, more immediate and tangible effect of the call. If selected, in a matter of days I would have to uproot my little family from a sleepy, safe, rural Wisconsin town to the fast-paced, urban lifestyle of New York City. My ever-supportive (and hunky) husband, Sean, had agreed to give up his job as Wisconsin's youngest district attorney and follow me to New York City, where he would take over my job as at-home parent to our then-four-year-old Evita, two-year-old Jack, and soon-to-be-born Lucia-Belen. I was both proud and scared at the thought of switching roles. Suddenly I would become our family's breadwinner, and with that came a different kind of responsibility. All three finalists had presigned contracts in the event they were chosen, and though I knew my income at *The View* would surpass the government salary we were currently living on, I had only the vaguest idea of the actual costs of New York City living. I worried whether my salary would be enough to live on. More than the financial repercussions of the decision, I was apprehensive about relinquishing the role I had grown to adore: being the heart of my family's life. I was sure that Sean, as helpful and giving as he is, could never duplicate my efforts as the family's "heartbeat," and with me working, I wondered about the impact this would have on all of us.

So that morning I let the phone ring an obligatory three times so as not to seem too desperate. I ran to our home office and shut the door so that Barbara would not have to hear the chaotic whirlwind of breakfast, *Sesame Street*, crying over spilled cereal and lost mittens, and everything else associated with getting hubby and preschooler out the door. I imagined Barbara Walters' morning routine: fluffy robe and matching kitten-heeled slippers, mimosas and personal assistants. I was sure my house sounded like total anarchy in comparison. I calmly said, "Hello," into the phone's mouthpiece, trying not to reveal any nerves (in case, of course, they were recording this to be used in the next day's show). A young woman's voice said, "Rachel, Barbara and Bill are on the line."

Barbara opened the conversation by telling me in that familiar, quasi-aristocratic, motherly way how "delightful" I had been throughout the audition process. Uh-oh, the setup. Trying hard to stay positive, I thought, "OK, they're doing the 'let's make her think she's not getting it' act." I started to feel sick. Was I even breathing? I heard Barbara's and Bill's voices but I wasn't really listening. Their voices sounded garbled, like the teacher in the *Peanuts* cartoons. Bill astutely figured out that I had yet to fully grasp the substance of the conversation.

Finally, Bill gently said, "We've decided on Elisabeth."

My graceful response?

"You're kidding, right?"

No, they were not kidding. It was painfully awkward, not least because I could sense how bad they felt. Though I wanted to make it easier for them and quickly hang up, I just couldn't let them off the phone so fast. I had to know *why* I had not been selected.

This was not my first audition with *The View*. When I'd first moved to Los Angeles, before I even knew what the *The View* was, agents, producers, and friends would tell me that I was a perfect fit for this new women's show and its chatty format. I was unabashedly opinionated and had an easy manner on camera due to the regular experience of candid interviews and confessionals for MTV's *The Real World: San Francisco*. Just as important, I was as passionate about politics and policy as I was about Hollywood gossip. So it was oddly unsurprising when I was flown to New York to have a meeting with Barbara Walters herself about replacing Debbie Matenopoulos in the show's early years. After a series of eleven on-air performances in the winter and spring months of 1999, I was one of two finalists to fill the slot. That time, too, Barbara and Bill called me at home to break the bad news.

So this call, just over four years later, was familiar, though very different. Just a few months earlier, Bill Geddie had asked me to return, yet again, to audition for the spot left open by Lisa Ling's departure, and placed me first in line among a list of more than twenty up-and-coming female hosts. I was certain that this time I was destined to land the job. I had changed so much over the nearly five years that had passed between auditions and had so much more to offer the show. Indeed, I firmly believed that every passing year as an at-home mother in Middle America made me a better cohost for the job! My Hispanic background and conservative values would also fill an obvious gap at the table, and many industry insiders thought so too. But most significantly, it was my real-life experience of living the life of so many of the show's female viewers that afforded me a perspective distinct from any other host on *The View*—or any other daytime TV personality for that matter.

And so I snapped to attention and peppered Barbara and Bill with questions. "What went wrong? What happened?" I really just wanted to scream, "What did I do that you didn't like?"

My thoughts raced from the details of one show to another to all the various encounters I had had with segment producers, executives, and the ladies themselves. I remembered that I had struggled with my lines once when the teleprompter was too far away for me to see. Was that the problem? Was I too aggressive in the preshow makeup room meetings where Barbara, Joy, Star, Meredith, and I (yikes!) lobbied for our favorite news stories to make it into the "hot topics" segment? Should I have concealed my assertiveness until *after* I got the job? I settled on an awkward green room incident where Barbara, reviewing my questions for an upcoming interview with conservative radio talk show host Laura Ingraham, told me I could not refer to Fidel Castro as an "evil dictator." Reminding Barbara that I was entitled to my opinion, Star Jones came to my defense (maybe *that* was the problem).

I looked up to see Sean through the glass of the French doors, bouncing a diapered and crying Jack on one hip. He had an unrestrained smile on his face. Sean was as excited as I was that morning. This was an incredible opportunity for me professionally, and I could tell that any misgivings that he had about moving to the Big Apple or becoming an at-home parent were outweighed by happier visions of paying off his law school student loans. Gesturing his curiosity with his free arm, he mouthed, "So what are they saying?" I looked at Sean's hopeful eyes and earnest smile through the glass and, dazed, slowly drew my finger in a line across my neck.

Sean stayed with me as long as he could that morning. He cleared up breakfast dishes and changed another diaper before reluctantly leaving for work, but not before giving me a sweet, fatherly kiss on my forehead and instructing me to "take it easy." He guided me to the couch and pulled a soft red chenille blanket over my body. I was an emotional puddle.

That day was November 24, 2003. That day was also my son's second birthday. I lay on the sofa, simultaneously feeling very sorry for myself and feeling very guilty about feeling sorry for myself. It was, after all, Jack's birthday. Consumed by self-pity, I was in no mood to bake a cake. My mother called, trying to be helpful. She has the no-nonsense perspective of many immigrants, and said firmly that this job paled in importance compared to the birth of her next grandchild. But even her good sense could not keep me from wondering whether I should torment myself by watching *The View* the next morning.

Sean came home from work and was surprised that I hadn't managed to pull myself together in the eight hours since he had left me. Realizing that I had done nothing to advance the celebration of Jack's birthday, he suggested we take the kids to their favorite place, the indoor swimming pool at the local hotel, order a pizza, and somehow make a cake. I protested and tried my best to convince him that we should postpone the celebration for another day or two. I lamely argued that Jack was too young to know the exact protocol for toddler birthdays. "We'll just tell him that parties are the day *after* your birthday." Sean didn't buy it. He hurriedly stuffed the kids in boots, snow jackets, and winter hats. He gathered their swimsuits and water wings into a plastic grocery bag, all the while pumping up the kids about what great fun we were about to have. They squealed with joy.

I was a much more difficult "project." Sean gingerly placed my jacket and boots on me, wrapped my fuzzy scarf three times around my neck, and forced me to march out to the car. When we arrived at the hotel, I protested once more, predicting pneumonia for the kids upon leaving the hotel with wet hair and venturing into near freezing temperatures. Giving in to Sean's determination, I entered the empty, chlorinated, and artificially humid pool area and helped him get the kids' suits on. Evita and Jack were ecstatic, and Sean quickly got in the water before Evita could jump in by herself. While they swam, I went to finally buy a gift for Jack and call in an order for pizza at Hugo's.

I reluctantly pulled into the large Wal-Mart parking lot. I wasn't in the mood to see people. Everyone in town knew I was up for the cohost position—the local paper had featured my selection as a finalist—and I dreaded the thought of someone asking me *tonight* if I got the job or not. I wrapped my scarf tighter around my neck and face. Maybe no one would recognize me. I climbed out of our SUV and braved the wind as I made my way through the slushy parking lot and through the heavy double doors of Wal-Mart. As I entered, I felt the rush of warm air and a sweet old man welcomed me in and kindly placed an empty cart in front of me.

When I looked up I was struck by a sea of blaze orange hats and camouflage-attired people wandering around the store. The day had gone from bad to downright weird, and now I was in some sort of Wal-Mart twilight zone. Suddenly, it dawned on me; I had spent so much time in New York City that month that I had forgotten that it was the opening of deer-hunting season, practically a national holiday in Wisconsin's Northwoods.

And then, like a ton of bricks, reality hit me right smack in the forehead. I live in rural Wisconsin! I, Rachel Campos-Duffy, live in rural Wisconsin. I am not going to live in a fancy penthouse in Manhattan. A driver will not be picking me up for work, latte in hand. I will not be dining in hip restaurants or be interviewed by E! Television on the red carpet or at the Daytime Emmys with Barbara and friends. I will not have an assistant, a publicist, or a stylist. I will not shop at Bergdorf's or exclusive boutiques, and I had better get used to this quickly! I shop at Wal-Mart. I was both depressed and startled by this news.

I quickly grabbed a gift for my son and returned to the car, replaying the events of the day in my mind over and over again. Even after I picked up Sean and the kids and we headed home, I remained distracted. Later that night, we settled for brownies with two little candles, instead of cake. We sat on pillows on the living room floor around the coffee table singing happy birthday to Jack, who could not have cared less if Mommy was on *The View* or not. He was so full of joy, clapping, smiling and singing happy birthday to himself before blowing out his two little candles.

As I looked at my beautiful son, something happened. Like floodgates rising, gratitude filled my soul, including whatever holes losing my dream job had made. The love I felt in that moment was real and overwhelming, and the biblical words "My cup runneth over" kept coming back to me. Somewhere between Wal-Mart and the brownies, my down-to-earth mother's words had taken root

inside me—the upcoming birth of our new baby *was* more important than any television job. And truthfully, being home with my
children brought me joy and satisfaction, something daytime celebrity could not guarantee. As exciting as the prospect of cohosting *The View* was, it would take me away at a critical time. Was it
possible to feel *grateful* for how things had turned out—*already*?!

The next day, I found that I *was* genuinely happy to be exactly
where I was: in my cozy house, with my gorgeous family, preparing
my body and spirit to bring another human into the world. The
travel and excitement of the past few months had taken their toll
on my pregnant body, and now, thankfully, circumstances had
conspired to slow me down, making it possible for me to enjoy this
stage, whether I'd asked for it or not. Sipping my morning coffee
and watching my kids chase each other around the house, I realized that I had been given a gift. Mothering young children, as any
wise grandmother would tell you, is a relatively short phase in a
woman's life, and I had a second chance to do it and appreciate it.
In the heat of competition, I had lost that perspective.

When Barbara Walters called that November morning, I an-
ticipated a moment of triumph. I had no way of predicting that my
rejection instead could be so empowering for my soul. That phone
call made me realize that I was **already** doing something worthy of
admiration, something that hitting the career jackpot would have
taken away from me. In my heart, I knew I was exactly where I was
supposed to be: home, savoring an irreplaceable stage of my life. I
wasn't going to get an Emmy for that role, but that did not diminish the power of it or how satisfied I felt in doing it (most of the
time). I do not mean to say that the end result of *The View* competition wasn't disappointing. It's never fun to lose. Nor did raising
two kids (now five!) suddenly become easy or unrealistically bliss-

ful. The difference is that in having almost traded it in, I was and am now better able to see the quiet and profound ways it brought me joy.

Like most mothers, I focus every day on doing the best job I can do. Lows are part of the experience but at the end of each day, the highs—those priceless moments that only happen in the intimate and private world of an at-home mom and her child—make all of it worthwhile. So I hold tightly to this precious and fleeting time with my small children with no regrets, confident that despite what others may think, my education and career experiences are not being wasted on my children.

For now, writing and blogging about parenting issues, and the occasional freelance hosting job, are just enough to balance out the work associated with the diapers, driving, and details of running a household. I have found creative ways to channel whatever energy I have left at the end of the day. I never imagined how much I would enjoy blogging, connecting with thousands of other mothers from my own bed each night. Today's at-home moms are constantly thinking outside of the box for ways to stay interested, informed, and connected to our passions and professions, while enjoying this transient phase of our kids' lives.

Stay Home, Stay Happy isn't about whether you should or shouldn't be an at-home mom. That path is personal to every mother and her family. Whether you choose at-home motherhood or, as in my case, it chooses you, *Stay Home, Stay Happy* shares the good news—at-home motherhood is a powerful mission, and you can carry it out with a daily sense of balance, joy, and adventure.

But like most adventures, it's always a good idea to consider a few precautions. This is the most important journey of your life, and *Stay Home, Stay Happy* provides practical preflight safety instructions that every mom can use:

"Good morning, passengers. Please ensure that your seat belts are fastened and your electronics are off until cruising altitude."

Yes, fasten your seat belt, Mom. You are in for the ride of your life!

"In case of loss of cabin pressure, masks will drop down from the overhead compartment. Put your mask on immediately before assisting others."

Naturally, parents recoil at that bit of safety instruction because it goes against our instincts—to help our children first. But it is a crucial step to survival. This safety tip applies to motherhood too. If we do not take excellent care of ourselves first, we cannot do our very best to take care of others. If we are running on empty, there's not much that we can give. *Stay Home, Stay Happy* is grounded in this simple yet often overlooked fact.

"In case of an emergency the exit doors are located . . ."

Sorry, ladies. There's no exiting this plane! Nothing can eliminate the turbulence, but with a few tips on how to take care of yourself, maintain your sense of humor, and appreciate the amazing choice you have made, you should be able to "sit back and enjoy the flight"—without having to resort to the cocktail cart!

Stay Home, Stay Happy sets out a few simple mom-centered principles that, if followed, can dramatically change the motherhood experience. By changing your perspective and taking care of mom's needs first, the inevitable drudgery that comes with the job (laundry and picking up toys and clothes are my personal demons) won't overtake the joy that motherhood brings. You can feel good about your days—even the parts that seem less fun can be more enjoyable. *Stay Home, Stay Happy* offers simple and practical advice that can transform the way you view your days, your relationships, your home, your mind, and your body. The fact is, millions of smart, educated women just like you are making the choice to be home with their kids. All of us want the same thing: to be there for our children without losing our sense of self and purpose. We want to transform the stay-at-home experience by finding innovative outlets for our creativity and professional interests so we can feed our minds and souls during this incredible—and fleeting—journey.

At-home motherhood has never been so good. This is not your mom's at-home experience! You are part of a new and growing trend toward at-home motherhood that has integrated and taken full advantage of the technological and cultural advances our society has made. The motherhood experience is so much more than it has ever been. Own it! And keep trying to enrich and enhance it for yourself and for other moms. After all, we know that there is nothing more consequential than using every part of ourselves—our time, talents, education, and experience—so that we and our kids can look back on their childhoods with warmth and wonder. With this book's help, you can rethink who you are, what you do and what you deserve. The decision to spend a large part of your day in the company of your children doesn't mean you have to lose yourself or your sanity in the process. It is truly possible to stay home and stay happy!

1

SAY IT LOUD, SAY IT PROUD

Celebrating At-Home Motherhood

- Ask Yourself: How Did I Get Here?
- You're Not Crazy: Validation Matters
- Self-Validation Makes Us Happy
- Take Ten: You Need Breaks!
- Dad's Appreciation Matters Too
- Taking Stock
- So Go Ahead, Toot Your Own Horn

A person may be proud without being vain.
Pride relates more to our opinion of ourselves;
vanity, to what we would have others think of us.

—JANE AUSTEN

~~~~~~

Pop culture has finally tuned into the fact that young women today are embracing, celebrating, and yes, *flaunting* motherhood in a way that past generations dared not. If magazine covers are any indication, these days no one can resist the celebrity "baby bump" watch. Entire Web sites are devoted to chronicling the latest details of who's giving birth and when. The current "mommy craze" and the public's fixation on motherhood are reflected in the rising number of women who are becoming at-home moms. However, despite trends toward at-home motherhood, even the most self-assured at-home mom can have doubts. The roots of this complex problem are many. Anyone, not just we stay-at-home moms, can get caught up in thoughts of the path not taken. After all, the grass always looks greener on the other side. We can become envious of the freedom we perceive others to be enjoying or the public recognition we wish we were receiving. Even in our own families, it can be difficult to get the respect we deserve for the work it takes for moms to hold it all together. How often have you spent considerable time preparing a meal or organizing a room only to find all your efforts going totally unnoticed? That alone can be depressing and cause a lot of frustration. And then there are those societal standards of achievement that sadly leave stay-at-home moms in the dust. Let's face it: tell someone who asks what you do that you are a stay-at-home mom, and the conversation is often over! But even though pride in at-home motherhood can often be a challenge, there are ways to create the support you need within yourself and within your family to make you a happy and proud stay-at-home mom.

Ask Yourself: How Did I Get Here?

Most parents have had some version of this out-of-body experience: you're casually hanging out in the living room or kitchen with your spouse and kids when your mind wanders off; suddenly, as if you were a ghost hovering over this familiar domestic scene, listening in on the various conversations, you ask yourself, "Who ARE these people? How did I get here?"

I met my spouse on a reality TV show, which for me kind of makes this moment even more surreal. What are the chances of a serious relationship developing from a chance encounter on a television show? I certainly would never have predicted that ten years later we would be the longest-lasting (and most fertile) couple in the history of reality TV (hey, *TV Guide* said so). But however exotic or mundane the origins of your relationship, when you spend the vast majority of your time attending to the details of running a home and family, as most at-home moms do, days just meld into one another, and it's easy to forget how we got here in the first place. And yet reflecting on that very simple but profound question may be all it takes to bring joy and satisfaction back into our daily life.

When I was in high school, there were most definitely a few girls who always knew they were meant to be at-home moms. They married shortly after high school or college and, well, pretty much got right to it. Most of my friends, though, came to at-home motherhood well into their careers, after a lot of deliberation and planning. They made a conscious decision, knowing full well the professional hit they were taking in order to be so intimately involved in the day-to-day, hour-to-hour development of their child.

In my case, though, it was more like at-home motherhood chose me. No noble deliberation on my part. It was simply something I was doing until my next big break in television came around. Before becoming a mother, I was an up-and-coming television host. When I became a mom, I was still trying to land a regular television hosting job after my first *The View* audition did not work out. I had a few short-term hosting gigs and truly loved this line of work I had unexpectedly found myself doing after graduate school. I had found my television niche! As a bilingual Latina host with a penchant for analyzing social and political hot topics, I was actively searching for a long-term job as an opinion-oriented television host. Thanks to successful stints on *The View*, I had had a taste and wanted more.

That was why after my first child was born, neither my husband nor I considered my staying home as anything more than a matter of logistics until my career took off. At that time, he had a paying job. I didn't. It seemed reasonable that the one who had a job or made the most money went to work and the other stayed home to take care of our baby. We were young and removed from the heated debates raging in the press and in intellectual circles. The "mommy wars" were in full swing but I had never even heard of the term.

Back then, I traveled frequently to Los Angeles for meetings and occasional freelance hosting jobs. I'd fly via Phoenix so my mom could get the time she craved with her granddaughter for the day or two I spent working and trying to put my career back on a full-time track.

However, with time, I began to identify more and more with my life as an at-home mom. It was like discovering my authentic self. I was falling in love not only with my child but with this new role. Gradually, it began to take hold of me, and though I was unaware of my transformation as it was taking place, I was, by the day and by the hour, growing into, loving, and appreciating this most undervalued of all vocations. Before long I began working my television ambitions *around* my desire to be a full-time at-home parent.

In the early days, during my trips to LA, I could still feel connected to my friends and my former life as a struggling single talent. And truthfully, in the beginning, I pined for my former big-city life and relished the excitement and freedom my business trips to Los Angeles provided. However, the more I traveled back and forth, the more I began to appreciate my life as a mom in the Midwest. Even during my time in hair and makeup—always my favorite part of any job—I was finding that I couldn't imagine doing even *this* every day, not if it meant missing out on what was happening at home. I wasn't worried about missing the milestone moments, the first step or first word. It was the moments that happened in that space in between, the space created by "quantity" time. These were the moments that I couldn't bear to miss: the funny conversations over cookies and milk, bath times when I could be convinced to just come in and play, rocking a child to sleep and being there when she wakes up, and even the opportunity to discipline on a daily (sometimes hourly!) basis. Yes, I even missed that most difficult aspect of my work: patiently putting a child in time-out for the fifth time, coaxing her into saying sorry, and giving a warm hug and "I love you" after. All of these experiences were shaping her character and conscience. I loved being at home with my daughter, but I always felt that something was missing: validation.

You're Not Crazy: Validation Matters

The sad realization I came to during this time was that the more I was coming to value and appreciate my work as an at-home mom, the more I understood how undervalued and ignored my work was by the culture at large. The more I poured myself into my family and viewed motherhood as the noblest of callings, the more invisible I seemed in the world outside of my home.

Many incidents bore out this suspicion. A colleague of my husband's once asked him, "What does she do all day?" Clearly this person thought I had a lot more free time than I did! Did this person think I was home watching soaps and eating bonbons? Another time, I was nursing our baby on a plane when I asked the flight attendant for reading material. She informed me that there were "no magazines, only *Business Week* and *Fortune*." Does nursing a child mean I can't appreciate a business magazine? "Hey, lady," I felt like yelling, "I have a degree in economics, you know!" It was becoming difficult to prevent my experience as an at-home mom from being tainted by other people's perceptions or, more accurately, misperceptions.

My sister was encountering similar problems. She was also a stay-at-home mom on an extended leave of absence from her career as a diplomat. Even though they talked regularly, her friends and colleagues no longer asked her opinion on world events or foreign policy. Instead, they would direct questions and comments on these issues to her diplomat husband, even when it happened to be *her* area of expertise. I realized that at-home moms were living the line made famous by Rodney Dangerfield—"I get no respect." Did people think we'd lost our intelligence or stopped reading the paper? More important, didn't everybody know the importance of an at-home mother's work!? Apparently not.

One afternoon, my mother-in-law called me from her cell phone. "Rachel!" she said urgently. "Turn on the radio. There's a lady speaking on NPR. You've got to hear it!" I turned on the radio and heard a woman discussing the common, basic need all humans have for validation and feedback. She went on to explain that this was the core of the problem for at-home moms. In fact, she said, studies that compared the satisfaction of working moms, part-time working moms, and full-time at-home moms found that at-home moms scored the lowest—the least satisfied. Why? *Because they receive virtually no outside validation for the very important and often difficult work of being home with their children.*

That radio show had an enormous impact on me and really helped me put my finger on something that had been troubling me. I did long for validation, but the sad truth was that I had given up trying to get it as an at-home mom. Isn't it ironic that at-home motherhood isn't afforded more respect in the age of Oprah, when therapy and navel-gazing hyperintrospection are at an all-time historical high? Nowadays, most adults are happy to tell you all about the impact, especially the negative impact, their childhood had on their adult life—so why such indifference toward those who have dedicated their days to giving children happy childhoods?

Well, bold social research conducted by a dear friend of mine, an at-home mother of four, may hold some answers. Judy was totally frustrated by the "conversation stopper" she perceived "at-home mom" to be whenever someone inquired about her occupation, so she came up with a plan to expose society's prejudice for *paid* work versus nonpaid work. At the next dinner party she went to, she told the guests she had a new job: household manager for a very successful land developer and widower. She explained how she was his "right-hand man," supervising and managing everything from his kids to his home. In addition to serving as family nutritionist, she was advising the widower on his extensive home renovations, dealing with contractors and design dilemmas. Plus, Judy, an accomplished athlete in her own right, managed the training and athletic schedules of his four very active and talented teenagers. Finally, she explained her role as family counselor, advising her employer on business and family issues, while serving as a surrogate mother to his kids, who came to her for advice on everything from dating to picking a college.

Judy couldn't believe all the interest and follow-up questions she garnered at this dinner. The successful "land developer" was, of course, her husband, and he listened with both amusement and disbelief as she executed this experiment on the unsuspecting dinner guests. But Judy felt vindicated. The guests were all fascinated by her "new job." By simply pretending that she was being paid to do all the things she does every day for her family for no pay, she was suddenly so much more interesting to other people.

Judy's experiment points to the primary problem for at-home moms. In this line of work, there is no salary, no raise, and no bonus—not even an "employee of the month" award next to the bathroom door to let you know that you're doing a swell job. Though a recent study revealed that the work of stay-at-home moms is worth $117,000 per year, there will never be monetary compensation for those who voluntarily choose to spend their days in the company of their offspring. And truthfully, that's OK, because money isn't what we're after. It's acknowledgment.

Common sense tells us that humans are wired to respond favorably to praise. It motivates us and sustains our interest and spirits. Lack of positive feedback and validation explains why full-time at-home moms often score among the lowest on happiness polls. So if validation is a component to happiness, and at-home motherhood offers none of the conventional means of bestowing approval, then how *can* you "stay home and stay happy"?

Self-Validation Makes Us Happy

The quest for validation can have damaging results. For example, some at-home moms become susceptible to "collecting" volunteer activities because they have bought into the line of thinking that being a good at-home mom is not enough, or that it is not worthy in and of itself. Of course, volunteer work is a valuable use of one's time, and certainly many organizations would flounder if not for the time and talents countless at-home moms contribute every day. However, if the purpose of volunteering is simply to garner the respect moms should already have for themselves, no amount of volunteering will fill that void. Moms who do this often find that they are overextended, burned out, and no more fulfilled than when they had no volunteer commitments.

Thus, the first step in being home and being happy is appreciating and valuing what I do. I cannot expect others to appreciate what I don't already honor in myself. After grappling with my desire for validation, I found that by answering the question "How did I get here?" I can quickly come to understand the purpose and value of what I do. Answering this question, initially coined in rhetorical frustration, became the essence of the process that keeps me centered.

Whenever I feel overwhelmed or down, I remind myself that this is, indeed, my *choice*. Unlike women of earlier generations, most of us have made a *choice* to be at-home mothers. There is real power in exercising choice. and I can accept that every choice involves trade-offs, including difficulties and bad days. I recall that I'm here because I love being a mom, I love my family, because what I do here—making a home, cooking a meal, mending a scrape, wiping a nose, hugging a child—***matters***! To whom? Well, to my family, of course, and ultimately to the world we live in. Our country, our world, are only as good as the families in them, and I am proud to be doing everything I can to raise joyful, kind, and confident citizens. But just as important and not so often discussed is the fact that I *enjoy* being a mother and derive pleasure from feeling like I am doing it well. This truly is the unseen piece of the puzzle. If the question is "Why did you choose to be an at-home mom?" the most fundamental answer is often overlooked. The vast majority choose to be home because they enjoy it and experience pleasure in nurturing their children and families!

And the trend toward at-home motherhood is increasing, thanks to tremendous improvements in conditions since our mothers' and grandmothers' day. From more supportive and helpful husbands, to technologies such as the Internet, cable television, and modern appliances that have freed up our time, mothers today can stay informed and connected to their passions, former professions, and the world at large. My mother-in-law recalls the social and intellectual isolation of at-home motherhood in the 1950s. For twenty years she felt like she wasn't up on current events and the world outside of her home. However, today, the ease with which I can access information, along with the flexibility of my schedule (Hey, I am my own boss), makes me and other at-home moms some of the most informed women I know. I have as much access as your average journalist to up-to-the-minute information on virtually any subject. I love politics and news, and I'm a C-SPAN junkie; well, I can take in congressional hearings while washing dishes, something office-bound employees can't do!

In addition, moms are no longer confined to our homes. Thanks to baby carriers, minivans, disposable diapers, and changing tables in public restrooms, moms and their kids can really get around! Trips to the museum, mall, or local ski hill can be made with little or no planning. This was not always the case, and too often, we take it for granted. But even though I can appreciate that today's at-home moms have it pretty good, I still experience lots of trying times when self-validation needs to go a step further.

Take Ten: You Need Breaks!

When the laundry is piled high or my kids are sick, I need lots of validation and right away! On those days, I ask, "How did I get here?" many, *many* times throughout the day. The work of motherhood can be mentally and surprisingly *physically* grueling. Like so many other things in life, at-home motherhood requires distance in order to truly appreciate it. Time away, even a brief time away, say to take a walk or meditate, is often all it takes. I call it "Take Ten." Yes, even as little as a ten-minute break can turn a situation around and help us shift our attitudes. As an at-home mom, you may have to get creative about your "take ten" moments. You may be able to convince your child to play in his room for ten minutes without you while you relax on your bed, sofa, or porch swing, or wait until your daughter is busy in the sandbox outside to do some meditative stretching as you look on. But many days you'll just have to resort to a Dora Princess video so you can have a cup of coffee while you check out the headlines or call a friend. These breaks are valuable tools for keeping your sanity and coming back into mothering mode with a refreshed and happy spirit. Acknowledging that I need and deserve breaks throughout the day helps me keep in perspective the fact that motherhood *is* difficult, that I am doing the best job that I can and that (on most days!) I would not trade my position for any other.

Unlike other occupations, motherhood does not come with built-in break times, and I can't always get away at the moment I most need it—say when the kids are getting on my nerves and I am in the middle of cooking dinner or some other task. In those stressful moments, I take a *mental* break! How do I do this? Well, I start by taking several deep breaths, then briefly imagine myself as an observer in the room. Here's the hard part: then I look at the "offending" child and try to remember the last precious thing done or said or some other act that made me proud. It's not always easy, and you won't always be able to "go there," but you can work at it so that you can achieve it more often than not and hopefully develop a powerful habit. I have found that in chaotic or stressful situations, taking a "mental" break, breathing deeply, and bringing to mind a positive thought—in this case about my child—really helps. Whether or not I succeed this time, my "moment" ends in a quick prayer of thanksgiving. It is a *privilege* to be able to spend so many hours in the company and, yes, service of my favorite people. For all its downsides (and there certainly are plenty), there is nothing else I would rather do.

When I model a healthy attitude for my kids and love them and myself through the difficult times, I feel proud. When I succeed at handling a difficult parenting situation, I experience deep satisfaction in return. These mental breaks have the added benefit of making me more *conscious* of how fragile and fleeting this time with my kids is, and they really do seem to give me instant perspective. Seeing my family from that vantage point, I can think, "Jack is really testing my patience, but I'm going to miss this one day, so I'm going to try to handle it positively!" These encounters with our children, both the good and the bad ones, are what really matter in life.

Dad's Appreciation Matters Too

Appreciating at-home motherhood begins with you, and you have every reason to take pride in what you do. That said, self-validation goes only so far. Even Mother Teresa got a Nobel Prize! I'm not expecting a humanitarian award, but the grind of running a house will deplete any good soul deprived of external appreciation. That is why, as a mom, it is important for your family to appreciate your role in this outfit. Even the worst of my mommy days can be turned around with a little recognition for what I do. It can be as simple as my four-year-old saying, "You're the best maker" (translation: the best cook). But for the most part, kids don't really know what you do. We often get angry at children for being unappreciative, but the fact of the matter is that they have no intuitive understanding of how hard it is to be a parent, especially a mom, and frankly, why should they? The only way they will figure this out is if they are told. And they *should* be told. Not so that they feel guilty, but simply so they can understand that their necessities and comforts are not supplied by magic wands.

So how do you foster a sense of gratitude and appreciation in your family for what you do? Well, it starts with your husband! The degree of respect and appreciation your spouse shows for your work as an at-home mom will be emulated by your kids. My husband and I make a point of praising each other's contributions to the family in the presence of our kids, even pointing out a specific action. For example, "It's so nice of Daddy to take time to help you put together your spaceship toy." Or "Aren't you lucky to have a mommy who makes your favorite breakfast." It's a very small gesture that has a lot of impact. For some reason, an explanation by the other parent resonates more, and that's part of why Sean's support is imperative to my happiness as an at-home mom. Thankfully, he's made it a priority to help our kids develop a sense of gratitude for what I contribute to the family.

While Dad's comments are best, I'm certainly not beyond pointing out my own contributions to my kids. The intention is not to paint myself as a martyr or look for sympathy, but there's nothing wrong with saying brightly, "Wow, look at all this laundry I washed and folded. I worked hard today to give us all nice clean clothes!" Believe it or not, this will sink in, so put it out there and give yourself your own due.

One day when my kids were very young, I taught them a silly song to sing for their dad as a thank-you for something he did for them. The idea and the tune come from the musical *Bye Bye Birdie*—except I changed the words. Instead of "We love you, Conrad" I taught them an abbreviated version, "I love my daddy, oh yes

I do. When he's not with me, I'm blue. Oh, Daddy, I love you." It was meant to be a onetime thing, but six years later, all the kids sing it whenever either of us does something nice for them, and I think in its own silly way it has encouraged them to take notice of the things done on their behalf and to express gratitude for them. I'm always surprised at how many times I hear the song in a week, and it has become such a family thing now that I like to believe that they'll still be singing it to us when they're sixteen and we let them stay out past their curfews!

The bottom line is that the degree of reverence and appreciation you and your husband show each other will be observed, absorbed, and copied by the entire family. As the at-home parent, you have accepted the position of highest accountability and personal sacrifice. In exchange, you are entitled to their utmost respect and devotion. It is very difficult to foster a sense of gratitude in your family if your spouse is not on board. You can't expect kids to get it unless your husband gets it first, and even good husbands can be clueless when it comes to understanding the scope of your contributions. Sometimes it's not even their fault. Ask yourself, did *you* really know what it took to be an at-home mom before you became one? The good news is that there are plenty of nonnagging ways to let him know.

For example, make a list of your activities each day and leave Dad in charge on a Saturday while you go grocery shopping, meet friends, or enjoy some alone time. Your list should include all the things you do for the household, not just the items having to do with the kids. Understand that he probably won't be able to do it all. The upside, however (besides logging in some much needed "me time"), is that you will return to a husband amazed by your multitasking abilities and far more grateful and willing to help out because hopefully he now "gets it"! This is just one tactic that has worked for me—I'm sure that you can think of others that might work for you.

Taking Stock

Taking stock of yourself is another great way both to get some good old self-validation and also some help from Dad. What unique talents do you bring to your family? Are you a good cook, organizer, or financial planner? Do you have a knack for interior design, gardening, photography, languages? And what about child care? Is your gift with the kids patience, compassion, or a fun-loving spirit? Here's a story about the power of taking stock.

When my first child was one year old, my husband asked me to consider applying for a teaching position at a nearby high school. "Honey," he delicately proposed, "we could really use the extra income." Though I didn't verbalize it, I was hurt by his suggestion. I thought to myself, "If I did that, we'd need child care, and you can't pay someone to do what I do." When Sean finished explaining the financial benefits, I calmly listed the qualifications my "replacement" would need to have.

"Well," I started, "she needs to be energetic, love children, cook breakfast, lunch and dinner, and be tidy. We need someone who is willing to do laundry, grocery shopping, and run family errands. Also, Evita loves to be read to, sung to, and taken to the park. Of course we need someone bilingual. Oh, how about a postgraduate degree?"

"Rachel," he responded with sincere desperation, "we can't afford somebody like that!"

"I know," I smugly responded. Before that conversation, Sean had never considered the breadth of talent and experience I brought to managing our home and caring for his little princess (truthfully, I surprised myself with my qualifications). After viewing my role from that perspective, he couldn't consider someone short of Mary Poppins herself!

Taking stock was an important step toward taking pride in my being an at-home mom. And making sure that my spouse was also aware of my "qualifications" helped him see that my contributions to our household were invaluable and, frankly, irreplaceable.

So Go Ahead, Toot Your Own Horn

As women, many of us are conditioned toward humility and we play down our contributions to the world as at-home moms. But of all my titles, none is more significant than "mom." Occasionally I am asked to appear on television to give my opinion on political or social issues. Inevitably a producer will ask me what title I want put next to my name on the screen. Am I a host? A blogger? A pundit? An author? A Republican? But why not mom? Or at-home mom, for that matter? In truth, this is the part of me through which I filter my view of the world. I am an at-home mom, and I cannot help but look at and understand the hot topics of our day from that perspective.

Too often we assume that others are far more interested in the work of the lawyer, salesman, doctor, or executive standing in the room than in what we do. Maybe they are. But maybe not. Frankly, I'm fairly confident that my days with five kids under the age of ten are more exciting and interesting than my accountant's or any number of other professionals'. Plus, I have the benefit of pouring my talents and education into people who truly love me.

So the next time someone asks you what you do, say it loud, say it proud: you are an at-home mom. Never, ever say you are *just* an at-home mom. You have the most important job in the world. Be proud of your noble occupation. Go ahead, toot your own horn! And do it without the slightest bit of reservation. Then, when the inevitable looks of admiration come your way, drink it up. There is probably no one in the room more deserving of it than you.

What's Your "Pride Quotient"?
Do you say it loud and proud?

1. You run into an ex-colleague on the street who asks what you're doing these days. You:

   a. Smile widely as you launch into a discussion about your at-home exploits with your kids!

   b. Apologetically confess that you are an at-home mom.

   c. Quickly try to list all your extracurricular activities, hoping to distract from what you are *really* doing.

2. When invited to a work gathering for your spouse's business, you:

   a. Excitedly accept the invitation for a night out.

   b. Run for cover—these types of events make you feel inadequate.

   c. Would rather have the night to yourself.

3. When asked what you do all day, you:

    a. Tell all gladly, the pleasures along with the "blood and guts"—you love every minute of both.

    b. Try to paint your day as happy and pleasant at all times—wouldn't want anyone to think being at home might be a mistake.

    c. Deflect the question and ask them about what they do because you would rather not bore someone with the minutiae of your day.

4. When someone belittles your job as an at-home mom, you:

    a. Let them know who has the most important job in the world!

    b. Get wildly defensive, but secretly agree.

    c. Feel sheepish and say nothing.

5. You often participate in activities with a lot of different types of people.

    a. Yes, because I enjoy meeting new interesting people, and I think they enjoy meeting me!

    b. No, who has time?!

    c. No, I prefer to hang out with other moms, where I am most comfortable.

Are you really proud to be an at-home mom? If so, are you displaying the attitude you want to project? If not, why not?! You are doing the most important job in the world, and you should let everyone know it. If you didn't answer "a" at least some of the time, then you need to reflect on why you are an at-home mom, recognize and appreciate the gift of your time in your child's life, and take more pride in what you do!

2

FEED YOUR SOUL, WORK YOUR BODY

Keeping Mentally and Physically Fit

- You Are Exhausted with Good Reason

- Get Inspired: What's Your Mommy Motto?

- Prayer and Meditation Create Inner Fortitude

- Exercise Makes Moms Strong

- Be Realistic

- 2 for 1: A Combined Approach

*O*ur body is a cenacle, a monstrance: through its
crystal the world should see God.

—St. Gianna Beretta Molla

~~~~~~~~~~~~~~~~~~~~~~~~~~~~~~

You Are Exhausted with Good Reason

At-home motherhood should come with its own warning.
There are few jobs more mentally and physically challenging than caring for children. From the moment you
wake up, you are in constant demand, managing schedules, meals,
chores, and feelings. Hopefully you have managed to build in some
fun. Thanks (or no thanks) to technology, modern moms are multitasking their way through breakfast, snack, dinner, carpools and
everything in between. Today's moms are the most efficient multitaskers in the history of mothering. In fact an AOL study called
"Global Moms" demonstrated that we pack an astounding twenty-seven hours of work into a twenty-four-hour day! Yep, when tasks
are broken down and individually accounted for (e.g., the phone
call you handled while cooking and bouncing a baby on your hip),

the average mom actually spends more hours than there are in a day meeting the needs of her home and family.

So while mothering is infinitely rewarding, doing it well calls for the patience of a saint and the energy of a three-year-old—especially if you are actually chasing a three-year-old around all day! Not many jobs require such a range of skills. At the end of so many days, my muscles feel sore to the bone, as if I had stepped out of a boxing ring. If the aches were the result of a boot camp work-out that was going to eventually lift my bottom and tone my arms, I wouldn't mind being sore and tired. Instead, it's another kind of exhaustion. The kind that comes from playing games, reading out loud (sometimes the same book five times in a row), changing diapers, wiping tears, breaking up fights, emptying the dishwasher, and loading up the dryer. It's the kind of exhaustion that only another parent can understand, and it's the reason so many moms get into a rut. Once the kids are in bed, most of us are simply too tired to do anything other than melt into the couch and veg out on mindless television. Plans and dreams of self-enrichment go out the window. If it involves anything beyond the energy it takes to lift the remote control, it's just not going to happen.

Well, I'm here to tell you, if moms want to do anything more than the bare minimum for both the kids and ourselves, we have to be fit, both in mind and body. With a little inspiration, we can get off the couch and start fine-tuning ourselves—both inside and out—to meet motherhood's challenges.

Get Inspired: What's Your Mommy Motto?

We've all seen those hokey motivational posters, like the mountain climber summiting over a bold caption such as "Dare to Soar" or

"Achievement." They may be cheesy, but Successories has been in business for more than twenty years because companies that need to motivate employees know that its products work.

That's why you need to find your own words to live by. Every day you hear, read, or get e-mailed great quotes and mottos. Start writing them down! Eventually, you'll come across one (or more) that truly speaks to you. Every mom should have her own spiritual or motivational motto that sums up her aspirations as a mother or defines who she is and why she does what she does for her family.

"Do small things with great love," said Mother Teresa. This has become my mommy motto. I love these words because to me they perfectly sum up the work of a mother. We do small things with great love all day long, but they are big things for the people we do them for. Whether it's helping my daughter dress and undress her Barbie (man, are her clothes tight!), or staying up late to make and frost cupcakes for my son's class, or holding a crying child after her brother has scribbled on her artwork, these are things that matter deeply to them. They are small things, certainly when compared to the life-and-death situations that Mother Teresa found herself in. But at this stage of my life, these are the small things God is calling me to do. If I do them with great love, Mother Teresa reminds us, they are no less meaningful to Him.

Find your quote or saying. Maybe you have not just one or two but several. Put them on the fridge or on your bathroom mirror. I keep mine taped to the wall next to my night table lamp so I can see it when I wake up and go to bed. I often use the quote as prayer. Some days, that short yet important quote is all I (can) say before I close my eyes, and yet I know that it means more to my Creator than any elaborate prayer. Other times, I can let my mommy motto be a springboard to deeper and more intense reflection. Find your mommy motto and let it be an instant pick-me-up throughout your day.

Prayer and Meditation Create Inner Fortitude

Prayer is to the mind and soul what exercise is to the body. Moms need prayer for strength and sustenance. We need to center our mind (and nerves!). When it comes to getting through our day successfully, prayer is as essential as food and water, and if we treated it as such (and too many of us don't), we would find that our days would start and end much more joyfully.

Prayer is important for many reasons, but as a mom, one of its most important purposes is that it allows for introspection. We did not choose to be an at-home mom to simply go through the motions of mothering. We are home because we want to have a direct and loving impact on our children's development on a daily basis. We want them to grow up in a home that is warm and encouraging and with a mom who is happy and emotionally present. We want to cherish this time with our kids because we know that it is fleeting and we want the whole family to look back on it with joy and fondness. Unfortunately, the day-to-day grind of managing a home can easily rob us of our original intention and motivation to be at-home mothers. We can simply become taskmasters determined to cross items off our to-do lists. Or we can find ourselves getting into habits of complaining (my personal Achilles' heel), or yelling, or nagging, or simply being crabby and self-pitying.

Praying at the beginning and the end of our day is crucial for moms. Prayer at the *beginning* of our day can help thwart the common pitfalls (being cranky, stressed, and just not much fun to be around) and get us off on the right foot. At the *end* of our day, prayer and quiet reflection allow us to examine our thoughts and interactions with our family and understand our triggers and bad habits. It can help us to identify problems and positive solutions for dealing with our kids and family. More important, time to pray and reflect at the end of our day gives us the opportunity to put today's issues to bed and offers the promise of a new beginning when we wake up.

But prayer does not have to be limited to morning and bedtime. I recall the chaotic days after the birth of my fourth child. Because I had two toddlers who weren't in school yet, the days were often grueling. It seemed that I could never get ahead. By the time I cleaned up after breakfast, nursed the baby, changed the diapers, and began to straighten up the rest of the house, it was already time to start lunch. And by the time I was done cleaning up after lunch, it was almost time to pick up my oldest from school and then start dinner. No matter how hard I tried to coordinate naps, it never worked, and it seemed like I could never catch a break. I specifically remember a rare day when I was actually able to get everyone down for a nap at the same time. The stillness that suddenly came over my home stunned me. "So, this is what silence is like," I sighed. I decided to catch up on my housework as I took in the peace and quiet. Sweeping the kitchen floor, I imagined myself a cloistered nun whose days consisted of nothing more than prayer and quaint chores set to the tune of Gregorian chants. The sound of a cranky, prematurely woken-up baby suddenly brought me back to reality. Who am I kidding? I thought. It's impossible to get "centered" in this house!

One day in the confessional I lamented my dismal prayer life. Father Henry, a middle-aged Franciscan friar with a kindly smile who always reminds me of St. Francis himself, listened patiently as I recounted my spiritual inadequacies. Then he told me something profound. He said that *my very life as a mother was a prayer*. That statement really had a tremendous impact on me. When I began to look at chores and time spent with my kids as prayers, these actions were transformed. The burden seemed lighter, and I felt more spiritually connected to God, my family, and my purpose throughout my day.

Slowly, I began to look at my work as a mom as "holy." I also began to notice that the days that started with prayer and meditation ended up much better than those that didn't. Now, don't get me wrong, with five kids under the age of ten, there's no guarantee—and certainly no candles or elaborate ritual involved. Occasionally, I can manage to get in five or ten minutes of prayer or spiritual reading before the chaos begins, but more often than not it's a simple one-sentence prayer as I descend the stairs to the kitchen to get breakfast going, asking God for the strength and wisdom to be the best mom I can be today. Small? Yes, but it's amazing how transformative it can be!

Making time for prayer and meditation is not as hard as it would initially seem. Too many people believe that deep spirituality is the stuff of monks or gurus or rich people with the time and money to tune their chakras and escape on journeys of self-discovery. How many times have I watched stars showing Oprah around their beautiful homes ("This is my 'spiritual room,' where I come every morning for quiet meditation before I do my morning yoga on the lawn.") and felt like a spiritual failure? It would be so easy to be spiritual, I'd complain, if someone else cleaned my toilet while I meditated, took care of the kids while I did yoga, and brought me a wheatgrass smoothie on a silver tray at the end of it.

Alas, the life of most moms precludes such luxuries, and if you are the mom of small children, you need to take your spiritual "breaks" when you can get them: while your toddler is on time-out, when you're driving the kids to school, or like me, when you're coming down the stairs to make breakfast. When it comes to your spiritual life as an at-home mom, don't wait for the "perfect" moment, or hold out to start until you have the time and money for a spiritual retreat. Start now, wherever you are, whatever you're doing, whether it's five minutes or five seconds. Prayer will give you and your family strength. Before the kids leave for school, I try to pray with them, even if it's what we jokingly call the world's shortest prayer ("Lord, I trust in you."), which is, no surprise, my kids' favorite one. I find that holding hands and saying just those five simple words gets the whole family off to a better start.

Prayer and meditation are very personal and individual matters. Your faith and heart will guide you. Since I'm a Catholic, my faith provides a framework and even centuries-old prayers to help me find my way. I also love free-form conversations with my God, but often, after a long day, I need some aids, and those ancient prayers are an incredible way for me to connect with spiritual mothers who have come before me. To help me, I keep little prayer books in my night table drawer; my favorite is a monthly publication called *Magnificat* with prayers, hymns, Scripture readings, and inspirational stories. Keeping small prayer books in a night table drawer is something my mother always did, and now that I am a mom, I understand why. It can be hard to get into a quiet mental space after a whirlwind day of kids, meals, homework, and bedtimes. A prayer book can take some of the "work" out of prayer and help you get into a spiritual state of mind.

No matter what your faith or how you choose to get in touch with your spiritual side, there are lots of books with short prayers or meditations and inspirational stories that a tired and busy mom can absorb and meditate on at the end of a long day. Make a special trip to the bookstore (alone!) and gift yourself one, or make yourself a cup of tea when the house is quiet and shop on the Internet book sites for a prayer or meditation book that really speaks to you. After climbing into bed exhausted, moms need to wind down, and prayer is scientifically proven to promote feelings of positivity and hopefulness. It also keeps us balanced and provides motivation and perspective for the hard work we do. You'll have far more to give to your family if you take time to take care of yourself from the inside out.

Exercise Makes Moms Strong

Exercise tops virtually every mom's lists of items that simply keep getting put off (and never done!). Lack of exercise takes a mental and physical toll on moms. When we don't do it, we feel tired *and* guilty. It's our downfall, even though we all know three very important things about it.

1. We need it to keep up with our kids.

2. Feeling fit and looking good boost our self-esteem.

3. No matter how much we dread doing it, we always feel better after we do it!

I firmly believe exercise should be a part of every at-home mom's day. Whether it's walking, running, biking, skiing, aerobics, or even rock climbing, do some form of exercise that you love or can at least tolerate. If exercise is not part of your day, you're probably not operating at your full potential—and you know it!

Most women, including myself, can give lots and lots of reasons for not being able to fit a workout into their day. I have many excuses, but the one that sidetracks me the most is my house. Instead of putting on my tennis shoes and jumping on the elliptical for thirty minutes while the baby's sleeping, I'll first throw in a load of laundry, pick up the toys—heck, even organize my sock drawer. Sure enough, by the time I'm finally "ready" to work out, the baby is awake, and the opportunity has passed. Over time, I have learned to overcome my procrastination by visualizing the end result—me feeling great after my workout! I have to remind myself that if I wait until the house is clean and in order before a workout, I'll never work out! Besides, I know that when I get off my elliptical to face the mess, the post-workout endorphin boost always makes it seem more manageable.

If workout success seems to be eluding you, and you have the financial resources, you should not hesitate to hire a professional trainer. You could even go in on it with another mom and split the hourly fee. A trainer is an excellent option for anyone needing professional guidance and that extra motivation and accountability. A trainer will determine where you are physically, help you set realistic goals, and track your performance—a worthy luxury for any woman. If you are thinking that you can't afford a trainer, consider this. When my sister-in-law Julie had her second baby, she wanted to start working out after six weeks of postpartum rest, but (like many women) feared she would procrastinate her start date. With her first child, more than six months passed before she started exercising again, and she knew: "Without having a set appointment with a trainer, I might not start to work out for many months." Her plan was very clever. She hired a trainer six weeks after giving birth for a one-month period. For a small investment, she had a definitive start date and a customized workout plan when the month was over. "Hiring a trainer was one of the best things I did for myself. At the end of the month, I could already see results and was well on my way to getting my pre-baby shape back. That was all the motivation I needed!"

If you just cannot afford a trainer, find a workout partner, preferably another at-home mom who won't mind the occasional crying coming from the baby stroller. Statistics prove that people who work out with a partner are more likely to stick to it. For moms who can join a gym or be part of an exercise class, there's accountability in meeting up with your class. When you don't show up, they say, "Hey, where have *you* been?" Also, there's the bonus of socializing and bonding with other exercise-minded people. Personally, I love the social component of being part of a gym, but with three kids still at home during the day, coordinating a babysitter (my local gym does not have childcare) is too difficult. In addition, Wisconsin can be pretty darn cold in the winter, and leaving my house in below-zero temperatures to work out is utterly unappealing. I know myself enough to know that I would make excuses and not go.

So working out at home is the way to go for me. After much trial and error, I have come up with eight tips for successfully working out at home.

Be Realistic

Know yourself and be realistic about what kind of exercise will actually work. My mother-in-law is an excellent cross-country skier, and when I first moved to Wisconsin, she offered to give me lessons. It took one session for me to figure out that as great a

Eight Tips for Working Out at Home

1. Commit to a time of day: whether it is before the kids get up, during their nap time, or after they go to bed, consistency and routine are crucial.

2. Keep your appointment with yourself: the dishes, laundry, and phone calls can wait.

3. Invest in efficient, motivating equipment: have options so you can mix it up and avoid boredom. I have a spin bike and an elliptical machine. For toning, I have dumbbells, an exercise ball and a Total Gym. I also have a Windsor Pilates tape.

4. Your exercise room matters: is it big enough? What about the temperature in the room? My cold basement became an excuse to skip workouts. I was much more consistent once I changed my workout space to a room on the second floor. Machines and dumbbells are potentially dangerous, so be sure to take your child's safety and access to the room into account.

5. Don't talk yourself out of a workout just because time is short: fifteen or twenty minutes of cardio, abs, or toning is better than none.

6. Put together several workout playlists for your iPod or stereo: great music helps workouts go by faster.

7. TIVO or record your favorite shows: if you only allow yourself permission to watch them while you work out, it can be a great motivator.

8. Wear cute and flattering workout clothes: they're not just for gym rats. If you look good, you feel good!

workout as it is, it just wasn't going to work for me. By the time I got dressed, gathered my equipment, drove to the course to meet Carol, and got my equipment on, I had lost my motivation. Moreover, I'm an Arizona girl at heart, and I hated the cold weather, no matter how picturesque the scenery was.

Even though I love the gym—it's indoors, so it's warm, and social like me—as a mom of five, I realized that I could not realistically be consistent about going because too many factors (babysitters, weather, inertia) could deter me from my trip to the gym. Instead, I took the money I would have invested in gym membership and purchased a top-quality elliptical machine (better than the one in the gym!). Between that machine, my old spinning bike, and an infomercial purchase I have never regretted, the Total Gym (the one advertised by Chuck Norris and Christie Brinkley), I can simply put on my sneakers and walk down the hall to get a full body workout. There's no drive time or parking problems. It's warm and I get to pick the television channel. In my case CONVENIENCE trumped everything! I also like having dumbbells and a balance ball around. If the kids are playing indoors or out, I can quickly grab either or both and get a little toning in while spending time watching them on the swing set or whatever they are doing. Usually, my kids try to join in on the "fun." My girls love any excuse to dress up, so when they see me put on my sneakers, they'll go get their leotards and start jumping and stretching. Beware: there's nothing like stretching with your eight-year-old to remind you of how much flexibility you have lost over the years!

Every mom needs to figure out what works for her and commit and invest in that plan. For some women, home workout equipment becomes a clothesline within a few weeks. They simply cannot motivate themselves inside the confine of their homes. The unfolded laundry or the dishes in the sink beckon them and prevent them from just getting to it when it comes to their workout. For others, exercise needs to be outdoors. A workout just isn't a workout for them unless they are outside taking in the fresh air. Other women need the encouragement and accountability of a familiar group of women in an aerobics or yoga class for motivation. If you are not currently in an exercise program, or if you are having trouble being consistent when it comes to your workouts, use the space below to write down the obstacles preventing you from exercising. Don't censor yourself; they're all legitimate reasons, whether it's money, an injured knee, or feelings of hopelessness. Go ahead, write it down. In the column next to it, write a potential solution. For example, your small children may be the reason you can't exercise. They cry for you during your workout or come too close to your stationary bike, which makes you nervous while you exercise. The solution may be to swap babysitting with a nearby mom. There's no cost, and you'll even get the added benefit of accountability since you'll be less likely to skip out when someone's planning around you.

Of course, one of the biggest problems moms have is finding

Problem	Potential Solutions

time to exercise. Melissa, an at-home mother of three and part-time photographer, gets up at five in the morning every weekday to go to the gym. At five a.m., the kids are still asleep, her husband is home, and she does not have to hire a babysitter. She told me, "I love starting my day out with the kids, knowing that my workout is done. I feel energized and good about having made time to take care of myself. Before I began working out early in the morning, I'd miss workouts because something would always come up. I need consistency."

I admire my friend's discipline, and agree with her that early-morning workouts prevent "life" from getting in the way of her program. Inspired by her determination, as well as her workout results (she lost more than twenty pounds), I tried more than a dozen times to get up before my family to work out. However, every time I set the alarm for six a.m., I'd hit SNOOZE and fall back asleep. "Just five more minutes," I'd tell myself, and then before I knew it, my more reliable alarm system—my kids jumping on my bed—would inform me that it was seven a.m. I'd always feel like a loser after failing to get up over and over again.

The reality is that I am, by nature, a night owl. I'm up hours after my family goes to bed, and I am alert and productive late into the night. I love the quiet at night, and it is my preferred time to write and blog. At six a.m., my body just doesn't want to move, and trying to force myself into an early-morning workout schedule only added more dread and stress to the workout proposition.

I began thinking about my college days, when I was in peak physical condition. In college, I could work out at any time of my choosing, yet I always worked out about the same time every day: around three in the afternoon. While three p.m. may be my body's optimal workout time, it is no longer an option since I have kids to pick up from school at that hour. But figuring out my natural "exercise clock" was very useful for me. Instead of fighting my internal clock to work out in the early morning and winding up disappointed in myself, I decided to exercise as close to three o'clock as I could. So now, after lunch and before my toddler takes a nap, I get my workout clothes on and commit to working out no matter what the house looks like. If he doesn't fall asleep at the appointed time, well, that's what Disney DVDs are for!

And don't overlook the simplicity of an evening walk to get your metabolism revved up before bedtime. I often see my neighbor and her teenage daughter walking the dogs after dinner. It's not unusual to see them arm and arm laughing as they make their evening rounds. It's a ritual that started when her daughter was in junior high, and has become an excellent way for Mom to keep those lines of communication open. With her daughter's busy high school social life, Mom sometimes finds herself walking the dogs alone, but she tells me that she can tell when her daughter is having school or boy trouble because during those times, she tends to make time for her evening walk with Mom. It's probably optimal to begin a walking ritual together *before* your child is a teenager. But no matter when you start it, everyone can benefit from exercise, fresh air, and an opportunity to bond as you take in nature's changing seasons.

2 for 1: A Combined Approach

I started out the chapter telling you that motherhood should come with a warning sign: "Don't even *think* about doing this without prayer and exercise!" Well, this truth led me one day to think about combining the two. I talked to Father Frank Folino, a dear friend and music aficionado who is well-known for his music collection, and asked him to help me put together a great workout playlist of Christian and inspirational dance and rock music. Not surprisingly, I loved his selections! By the way, if you have not listened to Christian rock in some time, it has changed a lot and deserves a listen. Father Frank's list also included Gregorian chants with techno backbeats. Techno chants have a great steady beat and rhythm that are perfect for workouts. Listening to these tunes while I work out is a form of prayer for me. It is also the ultimate in multitasking!

In all seriousness, it can be very profound to work your body, a gift from God, while listening to music that makes you think about Him. I have found that my workouts to Christian-inspired music have been spiritually powerful. Some of our deepest thoughts and clearest thinking can come during a rigorous workout, and I have experienced some incredible moments of gratitude during these times, for my health and for this moment to take care of myself. During these times, I have strong bursts of energy, and I find that time passes more quickly.

My Favorite Playlist of Spiritual and Quasi-Spiritual, Totally Danceable Workout Music

"Body in Motion"	Wiseguys 2001b	5:54
"Amazing Grace Dance"	Vickie Winans	5:45
"Higher Love"	Steve Winwood	5:49
"Give Peace a Chance"	Morel's Pink Noise	7:10
"Wake Up"	Dawn Tallman 2001	8:38
"Together"	Bob Sinclar and Steve Edwards	3:26
"Good Life"	Inner City Berlin Music	3:27
"Beat Box (Revision One)"	Beat Box Smart Bar	8:31
"Shake Yourself Loose"	Vickie Winans	4:48

"Fall Down"	Tramaine Hawkins	4:22
"Now That We've Found Love"	Third World	7:44
"Put Your Body in It"	Stephanie Mills	6:02
"Stretchin' Out"	Gayle Adams	8:09
"Today" (Remix)	Keith Edwards	4:52
"We Are Family"	Sister Sledge	3:37
"Car Wash"	Rose Royce	4:53
"Love Is in the Air"	John Paul Young	5:16
"Go West"	Pet Shop Boys	5:00
"Let's Dance"	Hezekiah Walker	3:50
"If You Need Love"	Tammy Trent	4:12
"When I Fall"	Rachael Lampa	5:09
"Dance Mix"	Nitro Praise	2:34
"Dance, Dance, Dance"	Mary Mary Gotta Have Gospel	3:32
"So Good to Me"	Keith Edwards	3:56
"Move Your Body"	Keith Edwards	3:26
"Tempus Est Iocundum"	The Soil Bleeds Black	4:03
"Everything Must Change"	Lynette Smith	8:40
"Heavenly Light"	Dawn Tallman	6:09
"Going Up"	Dawn Tallman	7:01
"Mind Body Soul"	Stephanie Cooke	8:50
"True to Yourself"	Diahann Moore	6:27
"You Are Why"	Dawn Tallman	5:58
"Believe (Brighter Days)"	Dawn Tallman	6:45

Music doesn't have to be overtly spiritual to give you this boost. I first became acquainted with spinning classes when I was in graduate school at UC San Diego. I lived in La Jolla and was a member of a small gym run by a couple of semipro cyclists. My favorite class was a nine p.m. candlelight spin class. In the candlelight, I could tune out the other spinners and concentrate on my breathing, my movement, and even my deepest thoughts. The music the spin instructors used at that late hour was different from the music played at any of the other spin classes. No techno or dance music. No jarring sounds. Instead only inspirational and even sensual music played, like the Gypsy Kings and other international musicians from Africa, Brazil, and France. The lighting and the music all contributed to a spiritual and even meditative atmosphere, and I always left the studio with a great workout and much more relaxed mind and soul.

We can all re-create this atmosphere at home, which may also be an advantage of at-home workouts. Maybe this is something that admittedly you cannot do every day, but probably everyone can commit to creating an atmosphere one night a week when body and soul meet for renewal. After the kids are sleeping, arrange candles or other kinds of low lighting in your workout area. Maybe you can add some incense or burn lightly perfumed oils. Pick the music that spiritually moves you and that's right for this occasion. Most important, what kind of exercise will you do that evening? I say, do not just try yoga or Pilates (which probably seem like natural choices), but try something a bit more active. I think you will be surprised at how easily you fall into the exercise groove while letting your mind float free to concentrate on other matters for twenty minutes.

The main thing is that at-home moms really need to take excellent care of their whole selves. But moms are also really short on extra time, so what better way to do that than to integrate mind and body workouts when you can?! Feeding your soul and working your body are both essential if you want to give your family the best of you. The time you dedicate to these endeavors is not only a well-deserved gift to yourself; you will discover that it is a priceless gift to your family.

My Favorite 80s Playlist

"Pop Musik"	M
"Rock This Town"	Stray Cats
"Pass the Dutchie"	Musical Youth
"Electric Avenue"	Eddy Grant
"What I Like About You"	The Romantics
"The Glamorous Life"	Sheila E.
"Pump Up the Volume" (remix)	MARRS
"I Can't Wait"	Nu Shooz
"Big Time"	Peter Gabriel
"Da Bump"	Mr. V Featuring Miss Patty
"What's on Your Mind (Pure Energy)"	Information Society
"Cars"	Gary Numan
"Upside Down"	Diana Ross
"Together in Electric Dreams"	Philip Oakey
"Don't You Want Me?"	Human League
"Fascination"	Human League
"Bizarre Love Triangle"	New Order
"Tour de France"	Kraftwerk
"West End Girls"	Pet Shop Boys

Classic Disco Workout

"Oh Yeah"	Bostich
"Souvenirs"	Voyage
"Move Your Body"	Expansions
"YMCA"	Village People
"Turn the Beat Around"	Vickie Sue Robinson
"The Hustle"	Van McCoy

"Boogie Oogie Oogie"	Taste of Honey
"Dance (Disco Heat)"	Sylvester
"Put Your Body in It"	Stephanie Mills
"Take Your Time"	SOS Band
"Get Up and Boogie"	Silver Convention
"Let the Music Play"	Shannon
"I Love America"	Patrick Juvet
"Hip Hop Bebop"	Man Parrish
"Funkytown"	Lipps, Inc.
"Rockit"	Herbie Hancock
"Best of My Love"	Emotions
"Groove Is in the Heart"	Deeelite
"Good Times"	Chic
"Got to Be Real"	Cheryl Lynn
"Ain't Nobody"	Chaka Khan
"Knock on Wood"	Amii Stewart

My "Current Favorites" Workout Playlist

"Just Dance"	Lady GaGa
"Feedback"	Janet Jackson
"Say It Right"	Nelly Furtado
"Human" (Pink Noise Radio Edit)	The Killers
"Pocket Full of Sunshine"	Natasha Bedingfield
"Together"	Bob Sinclar Featuring Steve Edwards
"Joyful Sound" (Wayne G 'Atlantis' Anthem Mix)	Debby Holiday
"Give It All You Got" (Bimbo Jonson Mix)	Ultra Nate Featuring Chris Willis
"Stamp Your Feet"	Donna Summer

"Turn It Up"	Mark Picchiotti Presents Basstoy
"I Love to Move in Here"	Moby
"Amazing" (Thin White Duke Main Mix)	Seal
"Relax, Take It Easy"	Mika Life in Cartoon Motion
"Above the Clouds" (Club Junkies Mix)	Amber
"Step into the Light" (Wayne G and Porl Young UK Mix)	Darren Hayes
"I Hate This Part" (Moto Blanco Remix) (Club Mix)	The Pussycat Dolls
"Grass Is Greener" (Radio Mix)	Dave Audé
"Single Girls (Put a Ring on It)"	Beyoncé
"When I Grow Up"	Pussycat Dolls
"Chasing Cars"	Fawni

Do You Need More Zen Moments?
Are You Properly Feeding Your Body And Soul?

1. You create a calming atmosphere by:

 a. Lighting candles and incense to soothe your senses.

 b. Taking a bubble bath with a magazine.

 c. Simply sitting down. Life is too harried to do much else.

2. The last time you had a good workout was:

 a. Yesterday!

b. Last month. You find it hard to carve out time.

c. Last year. You hate working out.

3. Inspirational words and sayings:

a. Really lift your spirits. In fact, you keep a few around to get you through tough days.

b. Are nice but you don't really read them unless a friend gives you an "inspirational" gift.

c. Are silly. What good are they? They're just words.

4. When you have ten minutes to yourself, you:

a. Clear your mind of all distractions and sit in silent meditation.

b. Read that article in *People* magazine you've been meaning to catch up on.

c. Panic because you can't stop thinking about all the things that need to get done.

5. Prayer or meditation:

a. Helps you to be better able to handle the demands of motherhood; you do it every day.

b. Gives you focus. You wish you did it more often.

c. Makes you uncomfortable; you are just not sure how to do it.

If you answered mostly "a" or "b," then good for you! You are well on your way to creating body and soul that will sustain you for your journey in at-home motherhood. If not, you can use many tips in this chapter to help keep physically and mentally fit to be the best mom you can be.

3

EMBRACE THE CHAOS, KEEP THE ORDER

Making the Most of Family Time

- Do You Like Your Home's Personality?

- Flexibility Keeps You Sane

- Show Your Kids Your Spontaneous Side

- Simplify!

- Write a Family Mission Statement

- Create Lifelong Family Memories

- Family Road Trip:
The Ultimate Family Bonding Experience

You can't save time, but you can invest it.

—UNKNOWN

~~~~~~~~~~~~~~~~~~~~~~~~~~~~~~

Total peace and serenity is a worthy goal—for **monks**! Not moms. If you spend the majority of your days in the company of babies, toddlers, tweens, or teens, then your happiness will be directly proportional to your ability to laugh often and enjoy the chaos. The child-rearing years, in particular, are meant to be hectic, playful, and fun! A large portion of your day will be spent in the company of little people with boundless energy and seemingly endless needs, and it can and should be enjoyable—if Mom embraces her choice and is prepared to make the most of it.

Do You Like Your Home's Personality?

Moms are the key to a happy home. The adage "If Mama ain't happy, nobody's happy" is as old as it is true. Every home and family have a personality, and Mom is a major determinant of what it will be. If we are happy and easygoing, chances are that our home will be too. If Mom is stressed and resentful, then that energy will inevitably permeate her home. What is the personality of your home? And how do you contribute to that feeling?

Taking time to think about the personality of your home and family is a useful exercise that can give you a lot of insight into who you are and who you want to be as a mom. If, for example, I want my home to be a place where family members can laugh and be themselves, then I need to nurture an environment where we don't take ourselves too seriously—and it needs to start with me!

I was stunned by how young my kids were when they started to make fun of Sean and me. Usually it takes the form of repeating back those parental catchphrases we all swore we'd never start saying. I walked into my nine-year-old daughter's room and before I could comment on how ridiculously messy it was, she looked up and said in a voice and cadence eerily similar to mine, "I told you to pick up your room before our guests arrive. Don't make me have to tell you again, or there will be consequences." It took me by surprise. For some reason, I thought my husband and I would have teenagers before the inescapable parental ribbing commenced. I felt so *old*. Mostly, though, I was sad about being pushed off my mommy pedestal so soon. When it first started, my initial reaction was to give the offending child a knowing look that said, "Don't go there." But later, I changed my mind. My kids weren't being *disrespectful*; they were simply being keen (and funny!) observers. Not taking myself too seriously has brought levity into our home because my kids learned that it's OK to be human. Learning to live with and laugh at our own flaws helps to reduce the stress of not always meeting our own expectations. Besides, sharing humor that stems from our imperfections binds us closer together as a family. This kind of humor is usually a loving indication of a family's intimacy. It says, "Of course you're not perfect. We love you anyway."

The ability to laugh in the midst of stress is an admirable skill that we should teach our children. Laughter helps us cope. That's why it needs to be in every stay-at-home mom's day.

Virtually every mom has had the experience of a child making a mess on such a grand scale that it could (and perhaps has) reduced us to tears. You know what I'm talking about. Walking into the bathroom to find your toddler "painting" the walls and sink with the toilet scrubber; or covered from head to toe in your so-expensive-you-almost-didn't-buy-it night cream. And yet the worst moments are the ones we will most laugh about when these years are long gone. One of my best friends walked into her baby's room to discover him in his crib, diaper off, finger painting the walls with his poop. Why wait twenty years to laugh about it? It's hilariously horrible right now! So laugh often and enjoy the daily bumps in the road.

Flexibility Keeps You Sane

Embracing the chaos requires flexibility because life with children is never dull or routine. Many first-time moms make the mistake of instituting strict schedules for naps and meals, and wind up unnecessarily frustrated when things don't work out the way they plan. They're tempted to pry their children away from a perfectly good time at a playgroup because little Johnny naps at twelve o'clock sharp.

Obviously, there are days and events that require punctuality and order; for example, when you have back-to-back dentist and hair appointments or the performance of *The Nutcracker* starts at two. But as at-home moms, we should strive to take full advantage of the flexibility that our choices and circumstances have afforded us. If we are at the coffee shop with our friends and all the kids are content in the nearby playroom, so what if they miss their naps or eat muffins instead of a well-balanced lunch? Enjoying a wonderful afternoon out with your friends and children is more important than the food pyramid, a missed nap, or any arbitrary rules we erect. Yes, Susie may be a little crankier this evening, so you'll just put her to bed a little earlier!

One true luxury of being at-home moms is that our schedules permit us a degree of freedom and flexibility others cannot enjoy. *Appreciate* this gift and take advantage of it. When the first snow starts to fall, drop that laundry you're folding and get everyone outside to catch snowflakes on their tongue. Remember that *this* is why you're a stay-at-home mom! Seize the moment because you know all too well that the nice trip to the coffee shop could just as easily have ended abruptly with an "accident" and a crying child with wet, drippy pants. Life with children requires that we live in the moment. When the moment is good, don't fix it! Go with it!

Being flexible and gracefully accepting the twists and turns that life with kids throws you will do more than help you keep your sanity. You are likely to find that it will result in more flexible kids, which is no small thing. And like it or not, you are your child's primary model of flexibility.

So, how do you model flexibility? When a stressful situation comes up (and they will), put it into perspective. Is it really that big of a deal? An excellent technique when the stressful situation involves your child is to try to react the way you would have wanted your own parent to react when you spilled the milk or came home with an occasional bad report card. When you're stuck driving behind Grandma on the freeway, don't honk and fume. Model the patience you want your child to emulate. Parenting from this perspective quickly yields good habits. You'll be amazed by how fast you will become the parent you want your kids to see.

Helping our kids to roll with what comes along has made life in our busy household much easier (and more fun) for everyone. We started early when, for example, we decided that absolute silence during baby's nap time would turn us into prisoners in our own home. During the day, the bassinet is in our open living room, where the baby is exposed to the sounds of a household in action. As you can imagine, our fifth child can practically sleep through a fire alarm.

In addition to modeling this kind of behavior ourselves, we try to "catch" our kids when they are being understanding and patient. Then we lay on the praise! Slowly, children begin to understand that you truly value these virtues, and they learn to value them too. If, on the other hand, you are highly regimented or allow them to be strictly schedule-bound, you deprive them of developing this useful life skill. Of course, we've had our share of meltdowns, but for the most part, our kids are learning to adjust well to whatever their circumstances, be it an occasional late night—like my niece's graduation party, where they danced their little hearts out till the wee hours—or an ill-timed trip to the grocery store, where they make an effort to deal by inventing games or being helpful. As the at-home parent, the one who deals with the kids the most, this is *crucial* to my sanity! Plus the whole family is happier if we all just learn to roll with life's punches.

Show Your Kids Your Spontaneous Side

One of my favorite childhood memories was a time when my parents did something totally unexpected and utterly spontaneous. As a military brat I lived most of my childhood abroad. When I was in elementary school, my family moved to Spain, my mother's native country. Our very fun Spanish neighbors, the Bielsas, became lifelong family friends in no small part because their three kids were so close in age to my three siblings and me. We spent many weekends playing while our parents hung out, laughing and arguing over politics, religion, food, and all the other topics that Spaniards love to fight about over good wine and good company. I loved our neighbors, but mostly, I loved that our families were such good friends because while the adults socialized, we kids were free to run back and forth between apartments to play and organize elaborate games of hide-and-seek.

One night, when our parents were up late hanging out, a discussion among the grown-ups about the Pyrenees in northern Spain resulted in a "dare" to travel that very night to the mountains and spend the rest of the weekend camping. They woke us up at three a.m. to tell us that our bags were packed and that we were about to go on a surprise trip. Our parents loaded us up in the car half asleep, but by the time we left the apartment garage, we were wide-awake and giddy from the excitement of it all. It was a great trip made all the more memorable by the spontaneity on the part of my otherwise very sensible parents. Even at that young age, I knew I was glimpsing a side of my parents I would rarely ever see—the part of them that was once carefree and wild. The craziness of it all humanized them in a way I would have never predicted. After that trip, it was that much harder to write them off as total squares with no clue about what it's like to be young and free.

That exhilarating memory always reminds me to keep the fun alive for our kids. There is so much darn scheduling and organizing in today's families. That's precisely why we need to occasionally mix it up and do something unexpected. It doesn't have to be an impromptu trip to the mountains. It can be as simple as an announcement after supper to "leave the dishes, grab your jackets, we're going to the movies!" Or a surprise reverse dinner where dessert comes first and the main course is last. These are simple things made more fun by the element of surprise. It reminds the whole family to appreciate the unexpected and live in the moment.

Simplify!

Embracing the chaos is all well and good, but notice I didn't say "*creating* chaos." Moms know that order also has a vital function in a family. In fact, the solid foundation offered by having a good general system allows you the mental space to be flexible and relaxed. And yes, *you're* the one who has to come up with the system. From scheduling activities to making sure that kids (and Dad) can find matching socks, I have accepted the fact that I am the front line when it comes to order in my home and that everyone functions better (whether they know it or not!) because of it.

A few years ago, I purchased a hanging office system from Pottery Barn for our kitchen (otherwise known as "central command"). It's called the Daily System, and you can customize it with a selection of organizational tools such as a pin board, dry erase board, and various cubbies for folders, pens, bills, and miscella-

Be Spontaneous!!

It's great to shake up the routine once in a while. Here are a few ideas to get you started.

1. Instead of eating at the table, have a picnic on a blanket in the living room.

2. Show up unexpectedly at your child's school to take her out for lunch.

3. Instead of going straight home from school, drop by a local diner for pie, an ice-cream shop, or any other place your child deems special.

4. Plan a surprise "date" with your child on a Friday night.

5. After school, surprise your kids with a tea party, complete with treats and Mommy's "nice" dishes.

6. Instead of staying inside on rainy dreary days, take a walk! (It's only water!) At least get out to a museum, a matinee film, or an indoor playground.

7. Have a kiddie cocktail party before dinner—make fruity virgin drinks and don't forget the little umbrellas. (This one is especially great for lifting everyone's spirits in the middle of winter!)

neous items I need in an instant like paper clips, a measuring tape, and the school lunch menu. It has been a godsend! Bills and school paperwork still get thrown on the counter, but now there's a place to put (almost) everything so we can find it later. I selected the Pottery Barn system because it matched my kitchen cabinetry, which was important to me since the wall we chose was large and prominent in the room. However, many other affordable customized organization systems online with features might make more sense for your family's needs. Whatever system you choose, consider this a well-spent investment in family sanity! If you lack the space or budget for any type of hanging system, then consider purchasing a family binder for holding all those school papers that can't be thrown out after reading, like lunch menus, practice schedules, and class phone lists.

Whatever your system, spending just ten minutes every evening going through the family's papers, especially the kids' school papers, is the best way to stay on top of things and avoid frantic mornings and the stress that comes from forgetting your child's field trip or snack day. Taking time in the evening to organize the family papers and schedule is one way I simplify my life. If you do not have a clearinghouse for your calendar, all the notices that come from school, the birthday party invitations, and the sports schedules, you are probably spinning your wheels and wasting precious time and energy.

When it comes to the family calendar, many moms swear by a handheld (such as a BlackBerry) that can electronically sync up with Dad's schedule; that way, you can avoid scheduling a family event during Dad's meeting. This year, I've resolved to go digital with my calendar, but I'm not giving up my trusty wall calendar because the kids like a large visual cue telling them what's ahead for the week and month. The truth is that displaying the family schedule has enabled my kids to save me more times than I can count when they reminded me about an event or meeting I had forgotten. If you have more than two kids, color-coding your calendar with a different pen color for each child may help. In addition, I like to highlight appointments that are of the highest priority.

If your family is overscheduled, however, no amount of organization will bring order to your home. That's why *underscheduling* should be a family goal. It won't always be attainable—like when your son makes the traveling basketball team—but it should be a family priority you strive to return to. Families need time to eat together and hang out without the pressure of always having to rush to a practice, game, or meeting. Take back your weekends! Nowadays they can be as stressful as the week. Buck the trends and restore its original purpose: to rest, recharge, and connect with your family. So many well-intentioned parents are cheering from the soccer field sidelines but can't find the time to sit down for a meal and have in-depth conversations with their children.

Today, it is not unusual for a child to be involved in three, four, or even five activities. We don't need experts to tell us that kids today are overextended and experiencing everything from depression to nature deficit disorder, often as a result of having virtually no free time to explore, play, or simply be still. Child psychologists also warn that the trend toward adult-organized sports is contributing to a decrease in many of the social skills kids once developed from neighborhood pickup games in which negotiation, leadership, and imagination were employed in the pursuit of *kid-generated* fun. The trend toward enrolling younger and younger kids in organized sports is resulting in injuries once unheard-of in tweens and teens. Still others are simply burned out by age twelve from years of soccer, hockey, or dance.

I first started to feel the "enrichment" pressure when my first child was three years old. As I waited in the hall during my daughter's dance class, listening in on the new and strange conversations of "experienced moms," I felt like a complete foreigner. I had never realized just how many extracurricular activities the other children were enrolled in: tap dancing, gymnastics, peewee sports, community theater, Kindermusik—the list was endless. As a child, I had never been exposed to ballet, so I had been feeling pretty good about being able to send my daughter to even one dance class!

How, I wondered, did these other mothers manage to juggle multiple activities for multiple children? How did they make dinner or help their other kids with homework and get everyone off to bed at a decent hour? It was a mystery to me.

I knew I didn't want to spend my days harried, shuttling kids from one activity to another, or resorting to fast-food dinners because there was no time at the end of it all to cook. But with all the mommy chatter about the benefits of so much extracurricular activity, I couldn't help wondering if I was shortchanging my daughter in the process.

Luckily, in short order, our two-year-old second child became a real playmate to our first, and I quickly decided that their playtime and bonding were more valuable than any preschool enrichment program. To this day, I reserve extracurricular activities for my school-age children and try my darnedest to stick to a sensible "one or two activities at a time" rule. Of course, every family is different and must make a choice that works for them; however, it's instructive to at least ask yourself if too many activities are a drain on the "life" of your family, preventing you from the together time you need to bond and truly enjoy one another's company.

When it comes to toddlers and preschoolers, it's OK to just say no to extracurricular activities. There will be plenty of time for "enrichment," but so precious few moments for the things that create lasting memories, like tea parties, dress up, and kitchen dance shows where Mommy applauds every leap and twirl. Now that I am considered an "experienced" mom, nothing gives me more pleasure than letting new moms know that they don't have to feel guilty for not going down the toddler and preschool enrichment road or

Ask Yourself If Your Family Is Overscheduled

Does my family regularly eat dinner together?

Are our meals generally nutritious and/or home-cooked or do we resort to takeout or highly processed "quick meals" because we are so busy?

Do my kids have plenty of time for unstructured, kid-generated fun?

Does my family have time to rest and bond together on the weekend?

Is my child excited about his/her activity or feeling burned out?

succumbing to the extracurricular craze for elementary and junior high kids. If your gut tells you that your family life is getting too harried and chaotic, it probably is, and it's time to simplify! No one wants to look back on these days as a series of car trips and sideline cheering. Choose activities wisely and be sure to carve out quality time for your family to be together.

Write a Family Mission Statement

Many families go through the motions (and work!) of raising a family without ever reflecting on its function, let alone the endgame. Writing your family's mission statement can help your family bring consciousness to what you are building and creating together. What's a family mission statement? Well, it's the same concept used by corporations and organizations to summarize their objectives. Likewise, a *family* mission statement is a brief summary describing your family's purpose, goals, and aspirations. It's an excellent way to identify who you are as a family, and what you hope to accomplish on this journey of life together.

The first step in creating a family mission statement is to convene a meeting to discuss and understand the concept. It's crucial for every family member to be present because in order for it to have real meaning, you need buy-in! In the meeting, family members share openly and honestly their thoughts on the current state of the family. Specifically, what do you love about it, and how do you believe it can improve? It's important to hear what individual members have to say and to listen and understand how *they* experience family. This is a wonderful way to know whether, in your family, communal *and* individual needs are being met. This is also the time to affirm important cultural, spiritual, and religious traditions as essential to your family identity.

Once your list is made, you will begin to get a sense of your family's unique path and mission. Look for overarching themes and references to specific religious and cultural values. You'll notice recurring topics and challenges in individual likes and dislikes. It may take several meetings to nail down your family's mission statement, but it is an exercise that can have real rewards. Think about it: when's the last time your family sat down to talk about what you mean to one another and what your dreams and challenges are as a family? This is a time to slow down and really think about *what* we are doing. When you do this, your family will have a stronger sense of purpose, history, and belonging.

My family first discussed the family mission statement over dinner. With pen and paper in hand at the dinner table, we asked everyone individually (including our toddler, who babbled a few things) to speak honestly about what they like about our family and areas they felt needed improvement. I have included the list we compiled here for you to see.

THINGS WE LIKE	AREAS TO IMPROVE
Family conversations	More sharing
Family dinners	No teasing
Checking in on our day	No yelling
Caring about one another's lives	More patience
Movie nights	More listening
Hanging out together	Less TV
Daddy makes money	More help with chores
Prayer time at night	Too much complaining
Encouraging one another's gifts	
Family dance parties	
Saturday morning breakfast	
Outdoor activities (sledding, skiing)	
Going to the cabin	
Lumberjack shows and logrolling	
No grudges	
Fishing	
Faith and traditions	
Open communication	
Love one another	
Lots of hugs and kisses	
Forgiving	
Christmas	
Being helpful	
Mommy cooking good food	
Taking care of one another	

From there, Sean and I synthesized these ideas into general concepts and drafted a mission statement for the children's review, suggestions, and approval. Since our kids are young, we wrote the mission statement ourselves. However, if your kids are old enough to get in on this part of the family project, let them! The more invested family members are in the development of the statement, the more meaningful it will be for them.

Now, the question is what to do with your statement once it is written. The first thing to do is to display it, preferably in a place of prominence in your home. Choose a place where everyone can see it and refer to it often. We put a copy of our statement on our fridge and another one, framed, near our family altar. Since everyone signed it, it can be referred to when explaining good and bad behavior to a child. It's equally useful for me! Recently, I was struggling to make a decision about taking on another commitment. Realizing that it didn't fit into the family mission statement I had signed made it easier for me to "just say no!"

It's important to revisit the statement periodically. Your family is a dynamic system with changing needs and demands. Your family mission statement should reflect this dynamism, and you will need to change or adjust it in order to meet your current family circumstances.

Create Lifelong Family Memories

Your choice to be an at-home mom reflects your desire to have a great family. You understand that a child is more likely to thrive and be happy in a family that spends quality and quantity time together on a regular basis. Sadly, nowadays, the belief that a child's heart truly desires to spend time in the company of his parents and

The Duffy Family Mission Statement

The primary goal of our family is to love one another and follow God's commandments.

We believe that each member of this family was chosen to be here.

We promise to treat one another and ourselves as "gifts of God" to this family.

Every day we will strive to:

1. Practice our Catholic faith and traditions.

2. Express our love for one another in words, deeds, and affection.

3. Spend quality and quantity time together in prayer, in play, and at meals.

4. Have honest, open, and good communication.

5. Forgive one another.

6. Do our part to create a warm, inviting, and clean home.

7. Laugh often (especially at ourselves).

8. Encourage one another's talents and individual dreams.

Signed by,

_____

_____

_____

family is countercultural. Through advertising, consumerism, and a media that rarely depicts a functional happy family, many parents are led to believe that the latest sneakers, video game, or toy will satisfy their child's heart. But it rarely does. Or at least not for long. Children want to feel connected to a family who values them enough to make time to be together.

Most families find that there is a natural lull somewhere in the week when everyone is (or can be) home. For us, it's Saturday morning and Sunday afternoon. On both of these days, I plan a slightly more special family meal. On Saturday, I make the kids' favorite breakfast (pancakes with strawberry sauce and sausage). After breakfast, we usually end up in the living room, where we finish our coffee while Sean takes song orders on the computer, playing everyone's favorite songs from our playlist as the kids put on dance performances for us. Later, we read or catch up on e-mail while the kids play or create "forts" in the living room. Sometimes we play with them, but other times we're just *there*, near them to answer a random question or share a story or joke that comes to mind. We all love it, and I can tell that those lazy, family Saturday mornings will be with my children forever.

However, if your family's schedule is extremely hectic or difficult to predict, you may actually need to carve out family time, schedule it into your calendar, and—here's the hard part—stick to it! Your family is worth it. If you decide that Sunday afternoons should be reserved for a big family dinner and some family bonding, recognize that you will get the occasional grumbling or even downright resistance for sticking to it. Your kids may need some time to adjust to this new event and/or slowed-down pace in their week. Try not to put too much stock in their complaints. I remember complaining about my school uniform when I was a kid, but secretly loving that I didn't have to think about my clothes during the week. These family rituals are the ones kids will thank you for later! I know, because I cannot smell eggs and bacon on the griddle without thinking of my *own* dad on Saturday mornings when I was growing up. If I woke up to Mexican ranchera music, my dad singing, and the smell of breakfast, I knew it was going to be a great day (even while I was displaying the requisite teenage "attitude")!

There are plenty of easy things you can do even on a weeknight. If my husband and I know we have an extra half hour after bath time, we announce that it's family spa night, and the kids squeal with joy! After their baths, they come in their bathrobes to our bed and select an essential oil for their foot and hand massages. After Sean and I give massages and if there's time, we also paint the girls' nails. It's simple, fun, and cheap.

If you have more than two kids, alone time with Mom or Dad is a treat in and of itself, and it doesn't matter if it comes in the form of a trip to the grocery store. One of my friends taught me a clever way to sneak "alone time" even on busy weeknights. After all the kids go to bed, one child is allowed to stay up for an additional twenty minutes with Mom and Dad, alone. I love this idea because so often as busy parents we think spending "special" time with our kids has to involve an outing. We're surprised when we realize that it's just our uninterrupted attention that they are longing for. When my friend first started this rotating system, the other kids had a hard time staying in their beds and allowing their siblings to enjoy their time with Mom and Dad. So, she implemented a rule that interfering with another child's alone time would result in a forfeiture of your alone-time turn. After the first forfeit it never happened again. During our kids' "special alone time," we read together or simply cuddle on the couch. When you have several siblings, having Mom and Dad to yourself is a real luxury.

One thing kids of all ages love to do with their parents is go through old family photos or videos. One of the cheapest fun family events you can pull off is a home movie night! Just pop the popcorn and bust out the home movies because kids love to look back at themselves as babies or toddlers, or remember what it was like to live in the old house or neighborhood. More important, watching videos together gives your kids a sense of belonging and history. Laughing and remembering when just brings everyone together and gives us a perspective on who we are and how far we have come. It's also a reminder of how quickly time passes. I always feel a little sad after watching home movies because I want to slow time down, but I also love that they remind me of how precious and fleeting this time is. I'm always left with a deep sense of gratitude for my family and the amazing times we have had together. As a result, both my husband and I have noticed an interesting effect: after a home movie night, we are more present and patient with our kids.

There are lots of other easy, fun, and bonding things to do with your kids, like start a garden and let the kids help select the flowers or vegetables. My husband started one two years ago, and in its first year it was a failure. The next year, however, he and the kids were at it again, and they had an amazing bounty. The failure of the first year made the success of the second all the sweeter. If you live in an apartment, consider a window box with plants or fresh herbs instead.

Everyone knows that kids love to bake. Why not make baking cookies or cupcakes a Friday night ritual? The memories of fun will last through the weekend with each bite! And how about an indoor campout, complete with blanket and tent? Our kids camp out in our screened porch with Dad because we've had several bear scares (man, did that freak me out!). They're safe on the porch, but knowing there might be bears out there makes it a real adventure!

You and your family can also take up a worthwhile cause to

work with or contribute to in other ways. Visit a nursing home, volunteer in a homeless shelter, or pick another charity project. I introduced my kids to a charity called Food for the Poor, which offers a catalog of things to donate, like a fifty-pound bag of rice, farm animals, or a school uniform and supplies. The kids pick what they want to save up to purchase, and I match every dollar they contribute. By looking through the catalog to select a donation of their choice, my children have learned so much about the plight of other children and the simple things they take for granted every day in their lives. More important, they're learning that even though they are kids, they can do something to help.

Sometimes it is the most basic things that we can do that are overlooked. For example, when is the last time you played catch, dolls, or cars or even picked up some crayons or played with Play-Doh? What about going for a walk or bike ride with your kids? Even though parents can feel like chauffeurs during the week, sometimes it can be fun just to go on a drive . . . especially if you finish up with a stop at Dairy Queen!

The good news is that there are lots of wonderful, simple ways to spend time together that do not require a lot of planning or money!

Are You Making the Most of Family Time? What's Your Home's Personality?

1. When someone accidentally breaks Mom's favorite vase, they can expect:

a. To be yelled at and berated for being so careless.

b. Mom to be briefly disappointed and then get over it. She knows it's an accident and doesn't want you to feel any worse than you already do about it.

c. Total confidence that your apology will be accepted. Mom loves you far more than the vase!

2. When your kids have friends over:

a. They avoid being around you because you are either not friendly to their friends or they say you embarrass them.

b. They feel comfortable that their friends are welcome.

c. They always end up in the kitchen with the rest of the family, where there's always plenty of food and laughter.

3. When family members have a problem with one another, they:

a. Give one another the silent treatment and wait for it to blow over.

b. Yell at one another initially, but later sit down to talk it out.

c. Discuss it at the weekly family meeting so things don't fester. Being in tune with how everybody is doing is a priority for your family.

4. At a typical family meal we:

a. Feel uncomfortable and sometimes fight. That's partly why we don't do it often or just turn on the television when we do.

b. Talk about one another's days and really try to catch up.

c. There's always a lot of laughter and conversation. Everyone looks forward to this time together.

5. When it comes to social gatherings in our home:

a. We don't usually have them. We are private, and hosting is a hassle anyway.

b. We invite our kids and their friends to be part of these gatherings. It makes it more fun for everyone!

c. Friends often remark that they love the "vibe" at our house. They can always count on good food and good company!

If you answered mostly "b" and "c," your home's personality is warm, inviting, and fun! Your kids are proud to bring their friends over, and their friends *want* to be there. You have created the optimal environment for building strong family bonds. If you answered "a" to any of these questions, your home's personality may need a little adjustment. Consider holding a family meeting so everyone can discuss how they and their guests feel in the house, and ask them to give specific ideas of what can be done to bring more fun and warmth back into the house.

Family Road Trip:
The Ultimate Family Bonding Experience

The time comes, however, when every family is ready for the ultimate bonding experience: the all-American family road trip! Traveling across the country with the kids in a minivan may sound like hell to some, but if you're a sucker for clean, retro fun and you're in possession of a good sense of humor, you've got the essential tools for enduring and enjoying this great vacation tradition. The singing, the fighting, the bathroom stops, and the messes in the backseat are the stuff of family memories. Traveling together, especially in a car, is a rite of passage that bonds and defines your clan as an all-American family. Our family has taken various kinds of vacations involving air travel, including a transatlantic trip to Spain, and plenty of short regional road trips, but there is no substitute for the kind of memories that are created by packing the family into a vehicle for a long *cross-country* adventure.

The first time we took a family road trip, Sean and I were amused by how weird it felt to be the "parents" instead of the kids. No longer could we identify with the perennially embarrassed Rusty and Audrey of *National Lampoon's Vacation*; now we were Clark and Ellen—but with a minivan in place of the metallic pea station wagon! The good news is that there are some upsides to being the parents, like being able to make all the cool stops we wished our parents had let us make. Thanks to the Internet, it's never been easier to chart out routes or get ideas about everything from snacks to roadside attractions to fun car games. Not only will time spent planning spare you unnecessary headaches so your family road trip can be the bonding experience you want it to be, but it's also fun for the kids. You shouldn't plan **too** much though. . . . Your trip should have enough time and flexibility in it to allow for unplanned stops and adventures along the way.

We like to let our kids get in on the planning because planning the road trip is half the fun! When the kids help plot the course, it really feels like a family venture. When I was a young girl, one of my older brothers was studying the history of California and the role of Spanish missionaries. My parents allowed him to select the missions he was interested in visiting during our West Coast road trip. He was so proud of his role in our trip that I believe it's had a formative impact on his love of history and travel. Our kids are still young, and if we let them pick our destination, it would be Orlando every time! However, during our longest road trip (Wisconsin to Arizona), we let them select from several different routes so they would have some say in the states we crossed. They wanted to see the Rocky Mountains, so we took a route through Colorado. We also tried to pick some great, hokey, retro stops—like the one in Moab, Utah, with the teepee and ice-cream store next door. It was right out of a *Brady Bunch* road trip episode!

Our kids get giddy with excitement before any family road trip, but it doesn't take long into the car ride before the thrill can wear off. Kids have a hard time figuring out time, distance, and trip schedules. You can cut down on the "Are we there yet?" mantra if you equip your kids with a custom map, a clipboard, and a highlighter. Then they can track the route as you go. Downloading a map and even a trip schedule gives them something to do in the backseat and helps them feel more actively engaged in the trip. If your kids are old enough, give them a guidebook to read about where they are going, and encourage them to share the information with their younger siblings, who can't read yet. If there is no guidebook that covers your route, download and print pages from the Internet and create a folder with a page or two about each stop or area you will pass through. They'll not only be educating themselves, but will probably educate you too, since with all the planning, you probably had no time to read up on it yourself!

Here is another fun idea. My friend Jenny has two kids, age ten and twelve. During each leg of the trip, she gives one child the responsibility for the family budget. So, for example, on the way there, her son Noah gets a jar with all the family money budgeted for the trip. When they stop for gas, Noah pays for it from the jar; ditto for the restaurant and hotel. After each expenditure, he calculates the new total so the family has a running tally of what is spent and how much is left. Everyone must come to Noah for money and he has (within reason) the authority to determine whether an expense should or should not be made. "It's amazing," says Jenny, "how frugal your kids become when they're in charge of the budget and can actually, physically see the money leave the family jar." It's an incredible way to teach kids about the value of money and what Mom and Dad had to save to make it all happen. My kids will soon be old enough to try this out, and I can't wait to see how they handle it. Jenny says her kids relished the responsibility and came back with a real appreciation for money and what their parents do to provide for them.

To keep up the mood when the road gets long and monotonous, we like to make playlists before the road trip with our kids. This little ritual has a threefold purpose. For one, spending time making the playlists gets them excited about the trip. Our playlists are an eclectic mix of kids' songs and songs we love—you know, really bad eighties music! Second, by making playlists, we ensure that when we do listen to music, it's together, as opposed to having kids on individual headphones, tuned out from the family. Everyone gets in his or her favorite tunes, and we all learn to appreciate the taste of other members of the family. The kids have learned to love Elvis and eighties rock, and we've learned to rock out to "Strawberry Short-cake" and the songs from the movie *Enchanted*. Finally, your trip CD or playlist becomes the sound track for your road trip, forever reminding everyone of the time spent together on this particular trip. In order to reinforce this idea, we try not to use the same CD for future road trips but make new ones each time.

For other entertainment, try downloading home movies on DVD for your car or portable DVD player. Kids love watching themselves, and I think it's a super family-bonding experience. Don't bother editing them because the kids don't seem to mind, and the raw, unedited footage is perfect for long car rides.

You will have a treasure for a lifetime if the kids document the trip in their own way. Consider giving your kids a digital or disposable camera. In addition, give them each a simple notebook, a glue stick, and some colored pens. Encourage them to collect souvenirs and to keep a journal at night, draw pictures, perhaps even paste some mementos in the journal as the trip goes along. When they return home, they can print pictures and complete their family road trip scrapbook. It will be a lasting memory of how they felt and what they thought at that particular time, and it will be interesting for you to see your trip through the eyes of your child. Sometimes you really have no idea what it is they consider fun or memorable. On our last road trip, our kids saw the Great Plains, crossed over the Rocky Mountains in a snowstorm, and stopped at a roadside stand to buy handcrafted Indian jewelry and take in beautiful desert vistas. When I later asked my five-year-old son what he most remembered from our road trip, he said, "Mom, for the rest of my life, I will never forget . . . Chuck E. Cheese's." Chuck E. Cheese?! Yup, an unplanned stop with Grandma and Grandpa for lunch at a strip mall in Arizona was the highlight of our five-year-old's trip. So much for the Rocky Mountains!

Great Road Trip Guaranteed!!

Keep your sense of humor and stay flexible—things are bound to go off course, literally and figuratively.

Get the kids involved in planning and navigating the route. Keep kids busy by giving them a map and a highlighter to track the route as you go. Give older kids a book about your destination to pique interest.

Make sure there is entertainment available for all. If possible, each child should have a small "entertainment" bag or backpack with books and two or three other items that they choose to bring from home. This is essential if Mom wants any time to herself in the evenings.

Food and beverage planning saves time and money. Keep a cooler with water or other beverages and snacks to eliminate unnecessary stops (and whining!). Research good "road food" along the route so you can avoid the usual fast food and try something more interesting (and probably healthier).

Document the trip with photos and film. Have the kids keep a journal and scrapbook. And don't forget to take video or photos of the car ride itself!!!

On a road trip, it's important to always remember that the journey is not only part of the adventure, but also what everyone will remember most. No matter how spectacular your destination is, twenty years from now, it's the time in the car that will likely define your family's memory of your trip. Why? Because being in close quarters with your family for long periods of time is bonding (even if you and the kids don't feel that way at the time). As an at-home mom, I find that making time to enjoy my family and facilitate new ways for our relationships to grow is gratifying. After hearing from friends whose tweens and teens want nothing to do with them, I decided not to accept it as inevitable. Maybe with enough family fun and tradition, my kids won't grow distant. And if they do, well, at least I'm spending as much time as I can with them while they still want to hang with me!

4

SHARE THE LOAD

Fostering a Meaningful Partnership

- Yes, You Should Have Expectations

- Communicate Your Expectations

- Switch Roles So He'll Understand

- Get Over It: Get Hired Help

- Put the Kids to Work Too!

*I*f we are together nothing is impossible.

If we are divided all will fail.

—Winston Churchill

~~~~~~

Yes, You Should Have Expectations

Times have changed, and men are more helpful and far more agreeable about pulling their weight around the house than in previous generations. We have our working mothers and sisters to thank for a culture that now expects men to help out at home. As soon as women entered the workforce in large numbers, the pressure on men to help out at home intensified. The effect this has had on the traditional gender roles attached to household duties has been profound, and both working and at-home moms have benefited from this cultural shift. However, for all this progress, one thing has not changed: unless women *expect* their husbands to help out, most won't. It's simply human nature!

My husband is not unlike most men his age. He believes that marriage is a collaborative partnership and that both spouses should help out at home and he does. Sure, it's not always fifty-fifty, especially when you are the at-home parent, but we've come a long way from the 1950s model of marriage where Dad's duties ended when he walked through the front door after a day at the office. The boomer husbands who followed were certainly more empathetic than their fathers, but didn't always deliver. In other words, they gave equality in the home a lot more lip service than action. On the other hand, Generation X husbands and dads deserve credit for actually walking the walk. An unsung story of the 2008 election was the prominent role of men in their families' lives at home. As a new generation of politicians came to power (the Obamas and the Palins), the nation was able to see in the national public arena what was already happening on the home front: truly complementary and collaborative marriages. Witness Todd Palin, Alaska's "First Dude." He is a blue-collar snowmobiling fisherman who is secure enough in his masculinity to hold babies and host teas for the former First Ladies of Alaska. First Lady Michelle Obama reported how her husband, while an Illinois senator, would return from D.C. on the weekends and resume his household duties of taking out the trash, supervising bath times, and doing grocery shopping and laundry. In the midst of his presidential campaign, he took a quick break to take his girls to school (once his regular responsibility) on their first day of the new school year, and continued to take his girls to school after the election. It may seem like a small thing, but pictures of the newly elected leader of the free world kissing kids as they head off to school was unheard-of only a generation ago. My own husband (a Midwestern lumberjack district attorney) is as comfortable doing the dishes with a baby strapped to his chest as he is wielding an ax or questioning a witness on the stand. Now that's what I call progress! These men understand that a truly successful marriage depends on true partnership.

In fact, a Pew Research Center poll found that respondents ranked the sharing of household chores as the third-most-important factor in a successful marriage. Faithfulness was number one, and number two was a happy sex life. That's right: a partner who shares the load is right up there with a happy sex life—and I daresay that there is probably a direct relationship between the two. I'm certainly in a better mood when I get into bed if I don't feel exhausted or resentful for having done all the household chores! The cultural shift in attitudes toward true partnership in marriage is reflected in the fact that in 2007, a full 62 percent of respondents said that sharing household chores was "very important," versus just 47 percent in 1990.

And yet, despite the importance of sharing household responsibilities for a mutually satisfying relationship, too many women have little or no expectations of their husbands when it comes to sharing the load! Why? Well, for those moms who have zero expectations of their spouse, chances are that they still undervalue their own work at home or believe their husband will never agree to help out. In addition, many of today's moms were raised by "supermoms" who did it all, inside and outside of the home. Their moms exhausted themselves trying to do and be everything, and felt guilty when they couldn't live up to their own high standards. If you were raised by a supermom, you may be having a hard time letting go of the guilt too. More than likely, though, you suffer from *my* "disease"—the one that tells you that your spouse will never be able to do it as well as you can, so you just do it yourself. You think, "Why bother? I can do it faster and better myself."

All of these attitudes are flawed and demonstrate something

very important about expectations, especially when it comes to dull and routine household tasks: expectations need to be *reasonable*— not too low and not too high—if they are to ever be fulfilled and make us happy. It is not reasonable to expect your spouse to do nothing (too low!). Nor is it reasonable to expect that you can do it all (too high!). Finally, it's not reasonable to expect your husband to do chores as well as you, especially if he rarely performs them. But that's hardly a good reason to let him off the hook altogether— remember, at first, you probably didn't know any more about household chores either. Like parenting, there's a lot of on-the-job training involved when it comes to cleaning and running a home. Let him do it, but be patient in the process! The bottom line is that if you both have reasonable expectations dealing with the unpleasant yet necessary jobs that come with living and running a home together, then you are statistically more likely to have a mutually satisfying partnership. Next time you both are at an impasse on account of who should take out the trash, ask yourselves what it's worth to your relationship. Chances are that a happy partnership is more important. Use that fact to inspire a compromise you can both be satisfied with!

It wasn't very long ago that "good" wives were expected to cater to their husbands' comfort and pretend that their days were undemanding. Maybe you saw this e-mail that made its rounds into many in-boxes, including mine, purporting to quote from a 1950s home economics textbook on how a wife should help her husband reenter the home after a long day at the office:

Make him comfortable. Have him lean back in a comfortable chair or suggest he lie down in the bedroom. Have a cool or warm drink ready for him. Arrange his pillow and offer to take

off his shoes. Speak in a low, soft, soothing, and pleasant voice.
Allow him to relax and unwind.

Thankfully, today's husbands do not anticipate these "comforts" at the end of their workdays. Frankly, if I did this for my husband, he'd think he'd walked into the wrong house! In fact, I can recall waiting for him at the door one evening with a crying newborn baby and the curt instructions, "It's your turn!" Not exactly June Cleaver. In truth, most nights he'll walk into a chaotic scene of me stirring something on the stove and an ambush of kids wrapping their arms around his legs, or trying to show him some project or paper from school. I love him and would love to offer him a more gentle entry to our home, with a warm drink and a soft pillow, but he's smart enough to know that I probably need it more than he does! That's because he and I talk often and candidly about our days and even about the unique stresses of a particular day (he may have a trial or I may have a sick child) so that we can support each other and also avoid unrealistic expectations when Sean comes home.

Communicate Your Expectations

Having expectations is only the first part of the story. Too often, women think men can read our minds, or at least notice that we need help. Neither is necessarily true. So the next thing you need to do is ask yourself if you are really *communicating* your expectations. Are you asking for help? If you don't ask, you don't get.

And if you are doing the chores without asking for help, you're probably building up unnecessary resentment. A story from my newlywed days illustrates this point. Six months into our marriage, I had finally had it! I had unwittingly taken on all of the household chores by myself because I like living in a clean and orderly space. But now the novelty of being a wife had worn off (that was fast!). I forced myself to stop cleaning the bathroom and dusting in silent protest. I assumed that Sean would notice, get the hint, and start helping out. He didn't. The dust piled up and before long I was disgusted by the state of our bathroom. Finally, after two weeks, I furiously cleaned it and waited for Sean to get home from work. What did he think? That I was his domestic servant? I was pregnant and tired and terrified that I had unwittingly signed up for a lifetime of cleaning up after this guy.

When Sean arrived, I collected myself and asked him to sit down on the couch so we could talk. Thankfully, I had cooled down and decided that I wasn't going to blow up. This newlywed was going to have a rational discussion that any television psychologist would be proud of.

"In five months," I began in a very controlled voice meant to mask my anger, "you have never, *ever* dusted anything."

"Huh?" Sean asked, clueless about what I was talking about.

"Do you think this house dusts itself?"

"Are you saying you want me to dust?"

"Yes!" I yelled. "And other things! I'm not your maid!" (So much for civility!)

"Whoa, just so you know, I don't dust."

"What do you mean, you don't dust?"

"Rachel, remember my law school apartment? I have never dusted."

"You've never dusted? You're saying you have never, *ever* in your life dusted? I don't believe you."

"No. I never have. My mom never made me dust. And just so you know, I'll *never* dust."

"What do you mean you'll *never* dust? Are you kidding? Do think I'm going to spend the rest of my days in Wisconsin dusting and cleaning your clothes and toilet?"

"No. I just won't dust. I'm kind of allergic to dust. I'll do other things, though."

"Well, haven't you noticed that this house is filthy? I stopped cleaning two weeks ago."

"You did? It looks fine."

"It looks fine?"

"Yeah, but if you want me to help out around here," he cheerfully added, "just tell me what you need."

This mundane argument over dust and household chores turned out to be one of the most important dialogues of our young marriage because it revealed so much about our true natures. For one, it revealed that I am a clean freak. And he is not. Like many other newlyweds, we didn't care about this important distinction until we lived together. More important, it brought into the open the resentment I had been harboring for months, thinking that he was expecting me to be his live-in maid. But my assumption couldn't have been further from the truth. While his mother never required him to dust, she was hardly a pushover. As the tenth of eleven kids, Sean was expected to do his own laundry, take out the trash, and cut, split, and stack wood to heat his family's home. His dad, though a hard worker and a remarkable provider, was not much help around the house, and Sean had witnessed firsthand the toll it had taken on his mother. While her load had diminished significantly by the time Sean was in high school (by then most of his older siblings were married or in college), Sean was familiar with the difficulties she had experienced in the early years, when she was running a home with eight kids under the age of ten and virtually no help with household chores.

More often than not, your husband is willing to help, but has no idea that you want something done. Communication is imperative. Take Sean, for example. Having heard his mother's candid accounts of the difficulties of being an at-home mom with little household assistance, Sean was determined to forge a true partnership with his own wife. Still, he was not sure what a "true partnership" meant. We had to sit down and discuss what each of us needed. If I wanted to have more help when he comes home from work, then I had to communicate my expectations in order for those expectations to be (mostly) fulfilled. On my part, I found out that Sean had his own particular set of boundaries, which of course included dusting and a couple of other things that he wasn't going to do no matter what. I accepted that, stopped getting angry, and figured out other things he could do to share the load and keep me from going crazy.

Talk about what chores you each prefer to do. Maybe he doesn't mind giving the kids a bath but hates to do laundry. While he bathes the kids, you can do the laundry. Or maybe you'll agree to cook, if he does the dishes. Here's where our complementary natures come into play. There are definitely household tasks for which Sean is simply better suited. During the winter in Wisconsin, there is a fair degree of outside work, like plowing snow and bringing in the firewood. These are tasks that an Arizona native like myself loathes. As long as there's a lumberjack living in the house, why would I do it? I'll leave the shoveling to Sean and cook inside any day of the week.

Don't waste time and energy wondering why he can't see that something needs to be cleaned. He doesn't. He's a man, and most men just don't see it. Of course, that doesn't mean that he doesn't want to help or shouldn't have to help, but if we want it done, we simply need to let him know. How many of your fights could be avoided with direct communication? If it's difficult to broach the topic of sharing household responsibilities, then how about writing up a simple list? Yes, a list is a practical way to avoid unnecessary tension and focus on what needs to be done rather than on why things aren't getting done—a conversation that can often go in the wrong direction.

Do not underestimate the gender gap when it comes to helping around the house. Sean willingly gives the kids their baths, but has never voluntarily picked up the bathroom afterward. Let's face it: this is another guy thing. It's the same reason holidays would be paper plates and takeout if men were running the show. We just have to accept that our husbands may not do things the way we, women, would. For example, when I make the kids lunch, it's a balanced, healthy meal accompanied by a little note from Mom on the napkin. When my husband made lunches last week because I was too tired to get up after a late night of writing, our daughter's teacher sent a note home telling us that she lent her money for lunch because there wasn't enough food in her lunch box! Oh, well, at least he tried, and we both got a good laugh about it. Discussing and accepting our strengths and weaknesses and our differences are a huge step in understanding and avoiding unnecessary conflict.

Always remember that no one likes to be nagged, and no one enjoys being criticized. The main reason men don't like to do housework is because their wives criticize how they do it! Humor helps keep things in perspective. Moreover, the ability to laugh about our differences keeps things focused on the task at hand rather than on inherent character and personality differences that are not likely to be resolved. There will always be things our spouses do that drive us nuts. Sean, for example, hates the way I drive, and I still can't understand why he can't put his dirty clothes in the hamper. If I point out that the appliances weren't wiped down after he "cleaned" the kitchen, he'll give me the playful reminder, "Oh, I didn't know you wanted to marry yourself." It invariably snaps me out of my pettiness and makes me laugh because there is so much truth in it. I really *didn't* want to marry a clone of myself, even if the clone would wipe down the counters. Of course, the same goes for him, and I dish it right back to him when he becomes impatient with my "grandma" driving skills.

One thing to keep an eye on: couples, especially new parents, sometimes fall into a pattern in which the mom does all the child care–related chores and the dad does all the house-related chores. It may seem like a natural way to divide the labor; you're used to providing the child care, and you may feel he's more trustworthy with the dishes than with the baby. But this is short-term thinking. In the long run, it's important to the parent-child relationship that Dad is as comfortable as you are caring for the kids, and that includes providing for their emotional and physical well-being, not just keeping a roof over their heads!

Switch Roles So He'll Understand

While it's true that men are evolving and taking on more and more responsibilities in the home, if you are an at-home mom, you may be at a disadvantage. Whereas working moms can at least hold up their paychecks and time spent at the office as a compelling case for an equitable division of labor in the home, bearing the title of the at-home parent can leave the impression that household chores are entirely your domain, even after your spouse gets home from work. Why? Because some spouses do not understand that you were *both* at work all day and that in fact your day was probably a lot more challenging and tiring than his.

Thankfully, my husband understands that no matter how stressful his daily grind at the office, my work at home is equally grueling. How does he know this? Because I share the details of my day after he gets home from work. And unlike the 1950s mom of the home economics book, I see no point in censoring or sugarcoating the day's trials and tribulations! Chances are that if your spouse is still unwilling to pull his weight around the house despite your having communicated your needs in a fair and reasonable fashion, he simply has no clue about what you do. So, it's up to you to let him find out.

If he doesn't get the message after talking it out, then you should try to switch roles. Yes, switch roles! And do it on a regular basis. Amber was a worrywart when it came to the kids. Even when she went to the grocery store in the evening, she always made sure that the kids were fed and ready for bed and more often than not she'd take the baby with her in case he got a little fussy. Amber was worried about the kids, but she was also worried about her husband, Drew. Could he handle two kids and a crying baby? Amber's reluctance to let Dad figure it out had unwittingly contributed to the undervaluing of her role as an at-home parent. Amber's husband had virtually no idea what her days were like and subsequently exhibited little sympathy for her requests for help. However, on the advice of a friend, Amber began letting go of her need to control and especially her desire to make everything better for Drew. She started to go on errands alone and occasionally out to dinner with friends. Alone with the kids, Drew had no choice but to make dinner, change diapers, and soothe a crying baby. Not surprisingly, it didn't take long for their relationship to shift. Drew gradually became more aware and appreciative of Amber's work as a mom, and Amber decided that giving Drew full responsibility for the kids, including the baby, for at least one full day a month was the key to getting more help and appreciation out of her marriage. No marriage is perfect, and some men may never become full partners when it comes to domestic duties. But by switching roles, at least he can never claim that he "had no idea"!

Are You an Enabler?
Do You Help Your Spouse Avoid His Share?

1. You're really sick and can barely get out of bed. You:

    a. Sleep in—your spouse has the lunches and the school run covered.

    b. Wake up just long enough to give your guy a few instructions to make the morning run smoothly.

    c. Summon your strength and get out of bed. Hubby has no idea how to manage in the morning.

2. The family is at a friend's house for dinner. The baby poops.

    a. You and your spouse flip a coin to see who gets diaper duty.

    b. Your spouse gets up to take the baby for changing. After all, you went last time.

c. You get up and change the baby. Why would you bother asking him?

3. Your spouse is in charge of dinner. You:

a. Can't wait to see what he whips up.

b. Hope he's followed your very explicit instructions as to what to make and how to make it. It took you an excruciatingly long time to write all that down.

c. Can't believe it because he has never made dinner before.

4. A girls' weekend away sounds:

a. Amazing! You want to pack right away.

b. OK, but time away from the kids is hard. You would really miss them.

c. Impossible. Who would watch the kids?

5. The house is in chaos. Baby crying, dinner boiling over, phone ringing, kids running around screaming. You need a hand! Your hubby:

a. Runs right in to save the day.

b. Runs right in to save the day after you yell, "Help!"

c. Goes to your home office to surf the Net.

If you answered mostly "c," your hubby needs to get a clue! And you have to stop letting him slide by without giving you the help you deserve. Sit down and talk about your expectations and how he can make your life easier.

Get Over It: Get Hired Help

Remember our "dusting" dustup at the beginning of the chapter? Well, one other important resolution came out of that discussion. When I realized that Sean hadn't noticed that our house had not been cleaned for two weeks, I knew that our very different standards of order and household cleanliness would forever haunt us. It was at that point that we both decided that our marriage was worth the financial sacrifice of hiring help. After studying our budget, we hired someone to come in once a month to do the deep cleaning. With Sean fresh out of law school and a baby on the way, this was no small financial consideration, but we knew that reprioritizing our budget to accommodate this new expense would go far toward taking this issue off the table. As our income grew, our once-a-month help turned into twice a month and then to once a week. Now, with five kids under the age of ten, I have someone come to help me clean twice a week for two hours a day. In the morning, after the older kids have gone to school, my hired help comes over and we clean together; it's like having my own wife! Usually, I take the upstairs while she takes the downstairs. Sometimes one of us cleans while the other takes on a project, like organizing the pantry or the kids' closets or switching out seasonal clothes. By eleven a.m. the house is in order, and I have the rest of the day to play with my kids, eat with Sean when he comes home for lunch, work out, and catch up with my e-mail and news on the Web.

My reasons for hiring help have evolved over the years. Whereas initially it served to smooth over a potential hot spot in our relationship, my primary reason for hiring help now is to maximize my time with my kids, family, and writing. Let's face it: most of us do not enjoy cleaning, and we can list hundreds of things we would rather be doing than household chores. So get over it! If it allows you more quality time with the kids, your husband, or yourself, and if your income permits, never feel guilty about getting outside help for cleaning, laundry, yard work, or any other mundane task.

Of course, I could just ignore the mess, but I'm a more efficient mom when my home is orderly and organized. With five kids, it's never going to be perfect; there's just a certain degree of chaos built into a family of that size. But with some household help, I can eliminate or at least minimize *unnecessary* chaos. Getting five kids ready for school, church, school programs, and any number of activities is a lot less hectic when shoes, hairbrushes, and homework can actually be found. And when things are in their places, it's also easier to delegate tasks to other family members.

In my book, lingerie and chocolates have nothing over help! Hiring help is hands down the best investment I have ever made in my marriage. It has minimized fights and resentment and freed me up to do what I love most. It has not eliminated the housework, but it has significantly reduced it. Now, when we do our family budget, household help is right up there with the electric bill. Sean and I both believe that it is a monthly expense that makes our marriage more harmonious, and therefore it's worth it! In fact, if given the choice, I would rather cut down on just about anything else.

I am a firm believer that women should never, ever feel guilty about hiring someone to help out with household chores. If you can afford it, do it! If you think you can't afford it, you may be shortchanging yourself. Before I reprioritized my budget, I also thought it was beyond our means. The really hard part for me was getting over the guilt and what I imagined people might say about it. Thankfully, it didn't take me too long before I got over it!

When my hairstylist, a single mom with two kids, told me that she was struggling to find a few extra hours a week to spend with her teenage daughter, I told her my story. By my next visit, she had hired a college student to come in and do her weekly laundry. It turned out that just that little bit of time freed her up for some mom-daughter bonding. "I can't believe I never thought of it before," she marveled. "I can't think of a better way to spend fifty dollars in tip money." And that's the point: my hairstylist felt great about her decision because she adjusted her budget to truly reflect her values.

The difference extra help has made in my day is equally dramatic. On the days when I have hired help, my day is easier, much more relaxed, and I have more energy to expend on the people and things I truly love. And I feel good about the fact that my values are reflected in the way my time and money are spent. Needless to say, when my mood and energy level are higher, my sex life improves. With that in mind, now sit down with your husband to figure out whether you can afford to hire help or not!

Put the Kids to Work Too!

Partnership doesn't start and end with your husband. Your family will be stronger if everyone pitches in. Both my husband and I grew up in homes where chores were just part of the deal. We both believe that our kids need the same responsibilities and we both make sure that the kids know what they need to do to help out. These days, however, we seem to be in the minority, with fewer families assigning chores. I remember a *20/20* story on families struggling with bratty kids. Hidden cameras revealed the kids throwing massive temper tantrums with very little instigation. A child psychologist was brought in to assess the situation, and he determined that the primary reason the children were so ill behaved was that they lacked responsibilities (chores) in the home. Despite his recommendation, the parents were all reluctant to implement chores, because they imagined that the whining and tantrums would get worse. To their surprise, however, chores had the *opposite* effect. After a short period of resistance, the children accepted their new duties and not only performed them, but showed dramatic improvement in their overall behavior.

Children want and need to contribute, and it is up to their parents to give them age-appropriate ways that they can feel personally invested in their family. Parents of small children often underestimate what they can do. My two-year-old, for example, surprised me with his determination to help me sort laundry. Since we have a front-loader machine, he can put clothes into the washer and take them out. Until he insisted, I didn't realize he could do it. Now the little angel, who happens to be a late talker, follows me around in the morning as I pick up and loves for me to send him on little "missions": "Please put these pj's in your drawer. Take this cup down to the kitchen." This little ritual has reassured me that although his language skills are lagging, John-Paul's comprehension, memory, and sorting skills are years ahead!

Starting children out early with small tasks that they can feel good about doing is the best way to nurture a habit of helping out. You may find that it helps to formalize those responsibilities with a chart. The thing is, parents know that teaching a child to perform a chore takes more time than just doing it ourselves. I can make a bed in half the time it takes me to teach my daughter to make hers. And I might need to make the bed with her a dozen times before she really gets the hang of it. But time spent helping your child learn how to sweep up, make a bed, or put away clothes is time well spent. You will reap long-term benefits for your effort!

And you know what? Cleaning up, especially for little ones, isn't always the bummer you'd expect them to think it is. A clever mom can always convince little ones to help out. Try framing the task as a "big kid" thing. Often, that's all it takes to make them happily volunteer. If they've wised up to that one, turn cleanup into a game. Set a kitchen timer (start with five minutes), and your child will work feverishly to beat the clock. If your kid has siblings, even better! What kid doesn't want to beat her sister?

You can also offer reasonable rewards. Most psychologists do not recommend tying allowances to the completion of chores; you don't want to promote the idea that the tasks are strictly for the employer's (mom's and dad's) benefit or that helping comes at a price. Rather, chores are for everyone's benefit, and we all do them to contribute to the community that is our family. You can, however, offer a "natural" reward. If the playroom is a huge mess, and no one claims it, I might point out that if the room gets cleaned up soon we'll have time to bake cookies afterward. That usually ends the finger-pointing and gets everyone working together pretty quickly!

So, What Can They Do?

Prior to twenty-four months, your child will want to help you (though it won't always be very helpful for you!). Don't discourage this desire to

help. These initial forays into cooperation are an important foundation for skills and attitudes toward helping later as children get older. Here is a list of age-appropriate chores. Of course, every child is different, and this is meant only to be a guide. However, you will be amazed by how much your children can actually do and, even more, by the fact that they may even *like* doing it!

2-3 YEARS OLD

Bring Mommy diaper/put in the trash

Help make bed

Put away/sort toys

Put laundry in hamper

Take items to various rooms in house

Help wipe messes

Put dishes away (if cabinet is low and dishes nonbreakable)

4-5 YEARS OLD

Set/clear table

Dust furniture/clean mirrors

Help feed pets

Help sort dirty clothes

Unload groceries

Help load and unload washer and dryer

Write or draw own thank-you cards with some help

6-8 YEARS OLD

Load and unload dishwasher

Vacuum and mop

Take out trash

Fold/put away laundry

Clean out inside of car

Pull weeds

Put away groceries

Take care of pets

Sweep walkway

Water plants (on schedule)

Make bed daily

Hang clothes

Help Mom with younger siblings (read, feed, dress, etc.)

Write own thank-you cards

9-12 YEARS OLD

Wash/put away dishes

Help prep meals or make simple ones

Rake leaves

Help babysit siblings

Clean inside fridge

Completely responsible for upkeep of their room

Help prepare for and wait on guests

> **13-17 YEARS OLD**

> Laundry start to finish
> Meal preparation
> Baking
> Grocery shopping
> Babysitting
> Iron
> Mend clothes

In the long run, your whole family will benefit when the kids help out. Moreover, you can feel good about raising kids who will be better roommates and better spouses for knowing how to clean. More important, they learn that relationships, marriages, and families function better when everyone cooperates and collaborates in the day-to-day functions of a household.

In our family, our kids know that they are expected to help. Both Sean and I work hard to ensure that our children fulfill their responsibilities. Together, we impress upon the children how important their contributions are to our household. Sean's support is imperative to my success as an at-home mom, not just by sharing the load but also by working with me to enlist the support of the whole family. His *true* partnership sustains my daily commitment to at-home motherhood, allowing me to feel even more satisfied and empowered.

5

REKINDLE YOUR RELATIONSHIP

It's Good for the Family!

• Pull Yourself Together

• Transitioning from Mom to Woman

• Schedule Yourselves In

• Plan a Getaway—Without the Kids

• Small Gestures Make a Big Difference

*I*f marriage isn't a first priority in your life,
you're not married.
—JOSEPH CAMPBELL

*A*ccustom yourself continually to make many acts of
love, for they enkindle and melt the soul.
—TERESA OF ÁVILA

~~~~~~

Time spent rekindling your relationship is not just a gift to you and your spouse, but a gift to your family! All parents struggle with finding time for their relationship. The demands of parenting, especially in the early childhood years, can easily have the effect of overshadowing the relationship between *the parents*. However, the health of the primary relationship has consequences for the family as a whole. Instead of thinking of the time you spend on your relationship as "time away from your kids," think of it as the gift it really is to them. Seeing their parents enjoy each other and support each other means kids don't have to be worried about whether their parents are OK. Instead, they can spend their time doing the things they really want to do! Your family will thrive and your kids will be more secure and happy knowing that their parents are in love and actively engaged in making their relationship, and family, strong.

Pull Yourself Together

Here's the good news: if you're an at-home mom, recent data indicates you are having more sex with your husband than working moms. So why are stay-at-home moms surprised by the findings? Because being home with kids doesn't always feel so sexy. When I lived in Los Angeles, and I was auditioning and working, it was practically my job to look my best every day. Whether you are a man or a woman in the workforce, projecting a crisp, attractive appearance is often necessary to your job. Grocery shopping and carpooling just don't quite provide the same incentive to spruce it up and look your best daily. Some days I don't know where the hours go. Before I know it, it's time to pick up the kids from school, and I'm still in my pajamas and a halfhearted ponytail. On those days I have no choice but to throw on a jacket and pray that the kids won't come to the minivan with news that their teacher needs to see me!

When you are "Mommy," it's hard to remember that you also have a name, let alone a gender! It's so easy to get into a routine of doing for others all day as our own needs slip lower and lower on the to-do list. It's a trap, though. Not taking care of ourselves affects our self-esteem. We need the confidence and energy that comes from feeling like we are at the top of our game. Remember the oxygen mask that you put on yourself before your kids? Taking care of myself by pulling myself together every day in simple, meaningful ways always puts me in a better mood and state of mind, which I find better serves my family. If we understood it for what it really was—a gift to our families—we might not be so passive about putting ourselves last.

It sounds simple, but just showering and doing your hair and adding a light touch of makeup can do wonders to pick up your mood, even if you have no intention of leaving the house that day. One of the study tips I was taught in college was to wear my favorite cologne or perfume during exams because an uplifting fragrance can actually alter your mood and improve your test scores. The same is true outside of the classroom. If I'm feeling sluggish and need a lift in the morning, a dab of cologne after my shower does the trick. I have also invested in attractive loungewear to feel dressed but comfortable, because pulling myself together also helps make me more efficient and energetic—it can have the effect of setting you on a productive and organized path for the day, as opposed to taking things as they come. Sometimes that's fine, of course, but if you need an energy boost, putting yourself together can definitely help. Believe me, I know firsthand how easy it is to slip back into schlepping around in baggy sweats and a scrunchie. As soon as I catch myself going there (and it definitely happens), I remind myself of how much better I feel when I'm pulled together—even if no one other than the kids will see me!

Splurging on bath and beauty products that make you feel pampered and sexy is an investment in your relationship. Don't be so darn practical! Remember how well you took care of yourself when you were single? Ask yourself why you are not doing it now. The reason is often because we don't have that motivation of trying to impress a man! We now take our husband's interest for granted. Or, if we recently had a baby and are sleep-deprived and/or self-conscious about our postbaby body, we may not even welcome his

Six Easy Ways to Pull Yourself Together Quickly

* A touch of lip gloss, mascara, bronzer, or under-eye concealer (I *love* La Prairie's Concealing/Brightening Eye Treatment)

* For more coverage, use mineral powder makeup (easy and looks natural)

* Ponytail or a great hat for bad-hair days

* Splurge on trendy sunglasses (hides bags and no makeup)

* Invest in one or two sweat suits or loungy outfits (fitted, not baggy!) for daily wear

* Fresh, crisp perfume or cologne (I love Jo Malone colognes)

interest! Even so, make taking care of yourself a top priority. Caring for a newborn can be so all-encompassing; this is precisely when we need to be reminded that we are more than just a food source! If you are sleep-deprived or depressed because your tummy suddenly looks like a deflated balloon, recognize that you can't really change any of those circumstances in the short run. Making an effort to treat yourself with some of the same tenderness you lavish on your baby can lift your spirits and maybe even improve your love life.

Perhaps there is a financial reason you are not caring for yourself like you should. In that case, find alternatives that fit your budget, but don't simply chuck it all because you're married and have a mortgage. If you can't afford a manicure or pedicure at the salon,

Six Ways to Pamper Yourself

* Exfoliate daily with a gentle cleanser
* Don't skip your haircut and color appointments—there's no substitute for that right-out-of-the-salon hair feeling!
* Monthly facial (You can do it yourself! See chapter nine)
* Luxurious bath products
* Manicure/pedicure
* Massage

give yourself one. Plus, some things are free—it doesn't cost a dime to tweeze your eyebrows (I'm assuming you already own tweezers). If your eyebrows aren't groomed, it's not your budget that's holding you back. You probably just stopped caring about them. Why? Your eyes are the windows to your soul. Why not bring attention to them?

Other products and treatments do cost, and you will have to decide if they are worth your time and money. I bought a foot spa to soak and massage my feet. Yes, there was an initial cost, but the purchase has saved me the repeated expense (and time) of going elsewhere. The important thing here is to understand that as a woman, you should have some type of beauty regimen that works for you. There is *nothing* attractive about becoming as practical and low-maintenance as a man!

Transitioning from Mom to Woman

When it comes to romance, the biggest obstacle for at-home moms is that our work doesn't provide a transition. How many of us have found ourselves bewildered by a gleam in our husband's eyes upon his coming home from work? How can he be thinking about *that* with the kids screaming, spaghetti sauce boiling over, and baby food splattered all over your shirt? More often than not, by the end of the day, I couldn't feel more UNsexy!

Why the difference? Well, part of the answer is that men are simply wired differently (and they find our messy hair sexy!). But another good part of the reason is that he's had some downtime on the way home to transition out of work mode. Hopefully he's had some time to decompress and put work stresses behind him for the evening, or maybe he's still stressed out and looking forward to coming home to relax. Either way, for him, home is a respite. But you, you're still at "the office"! If you don't create some transition for yourself, it's hard to meet your husband where he's at emotionally or physically.

The good news is that a transition from total mommy mode to "woman" mode is not that hard, and you can both help make it happen. If you can, find time *before* your husband comes home to do something relaxing (read a magazine, file your nails, play or color with the kids). I have to admit, I find that pretty much impossible. It's too hectic in the afternoon after I pick up kids from school. I get everyone in the house, make a snack, and get them started on their homework. Then it's time to start dealing with dinner. If your schedule is like mine, you'll need to enlist your husband's help when he comes home so that you can unwind.

One of my friends occasionally calls her husband and tells him to leave the car running when he gets home. When he walks in, she gives him a peck and a cheery greeting, and immediately leaves the house to climb into his warm car for a ten-minute drive. When she gets back, the kids have settled down from the excitement of Dad coming home, and she's in a much better mood for dinner and whatever else might happen! I'm blown away by how in tune she is with herself. She recognizes the need she has for a transition, and she takes responsibility for it and makes it happen! The trick, she says, is to make a quick and painless exit. Otherwise, it's all too easy to get sidetracked and lose your moment for a short getaway.

Here's how I coordinate my transition from mom to "Rachel" with my husband. Instead of before dinner, I transition after the kids are settled for bed. I'll give the baby to Sean and sit by the fire and decompress. Sometimes I need more time than that! So I ask Sean to do bedtime by himself, and I escape to the bathtub with a magazine and candles. It's really hard to describe what a warm bath, shaved legs, and soft skin can do to make you feel like a woman again. I know I've been really crabby when Sean draws the bath without asking me and practically pushes me into the bathroom for some "forced" relaxation!

Whether we work from home or are full-time moms, being home all day can make it hard to feel like we're ever off duty. That's why rituals can help us to transition out of our "work mode" and into a more relaxed, and potentially romantic, state.

It's important to get out of Mommy mode sometimes so we don't forget to relate to our husbands adult to adult, and not just parent to parent. We all have more than one facet! Your relationship will be much better if you have things to discuss besides your kids, and if you're both reminded why you ever liked each other in the first place! The whole family will benefit if your love life is in balance. I'm not just talking about S-E-X. You will be a happier,

Six Ways to Transition Out of "Mom" Mode

* A glass of wine

* A workout followed by a refreshing shower

* A warm bath

* A walk or drive

* Fifteen minutes alone with a book or magazine

* Call a friend to talk about nothing in particular

better mom, and your children will flourish, when your relationship with your partner is loving. There is simply no shortage of research that confirms the healthy emotional benefits a strong and loving marriage has on children. But we really don't need research to tell us that—we know it intuitively and anecdotally. Think back on your own family memories. Weren't you happier and more contented when you were basking in the love between your parents? And conversely, weren't you more anxious and insecure when you knew they were fighting? That's why young kids love it so much when their parents kiss and hug each other. It's proof that they are cushioned by a loving family unit. It's the kind of reassurance kids need to feel secure and happy. When my own kids see us kiss, they invariably act grossed out. They grab their throats like they're choking or make vomiting sounds and try to separate us. Our four-year-old will declare that "this is soooo 'usgusting!" But I can assure you that *all* of them actually love it. The smiles on their faces give them away. In fact, we keep the fun going by exaggerating our kisses, Hollywood-style, which really gets them riled up. Understand, though, that by the time your kids are teens, they'll actually *mean* it when they tell you to stop. So if your kids are young like mine, enjoy the PDA while you can!

Schedule Yourselves In

Scheduling regular date nights says "our relationship matters," and by making it a regular affair, you can minimize scheduling conflicts with your partner and with your child-care provider. If you're lucky enough to have grandparents who help out, they probably appreciate knowing that Saturday night is reserved for the grandkids. If you don't have relatives who can help out and you can't afford a weekly sitter, find another couple with whom you can trade off or barter in some other way.

Getting dolled up for a night out with my husband or with another couple is one way to date. I also love to schedule dates during the day. Our hometown of Ashland has a great coffee shop; occasionally we book a babysitter on a Saturday morning and spend a couple of hours there, reading the paper and socializing. For some reason, hanging out in that environment without the interruption of kids takes me back to my college days. I always feel a little more carefree afterward. Other times, we go out for breakfast alone, something that is uniquely romantic for us because our first real date was breakfast at a diner in Saint Paul, Minnesota. Now, our favorite breakfast joint getaway is the Delta Diner, a 1950s-style diner-car restaurant twenty minutes outside of town. It's in the middle of nowhere, and I always get a kick out of seeing how many cars are parked out front when there is nothing but woods and farms as far as the eye can see.

If you have relatives or friends willing to keep your kids for the evening or, better yet, the night, there can be nothing better than a night alone in your own house. Last year, we had an unexpected week alone in our house, and it was divine. It was the week I was due to have our fifth baby. My two youngest kids were in Arizona with their grandparents and the two oldest were in school during the day. Sean had taken the week off in anticipation of our due date. For five whole days we were alone together. After the kids went to school, we'd have coffee and read the paper, hang out, and go on walks. Toward the end of the week, we drove out to the Delta Diner for a late breakfast in hopes that the bumpy back roads might finally do the trick and get my labor moving along. Knowing that another round of sleepless nights awaited us once the baby was born made us savor and appreciate these long, unscheduled days together—it was truly a rare treat. Despite my swollen belly, it was extremely romantic to be reminded of how much we still love to just be together. It's what we loved to do before we got married, and here we were, waiting on baby number five, and still excited about just being able to hang out together. Taking a vacation day during the week while your kids are busy at school is an excellent way for couples to get alone time. You can go out to lunch together, hit a matinee, or just hang out at home and do all the things you *can't* do when the kids are around.

Does Your Relationship Need Rekindling?
Are You "Showing Up" for Your Relationship?

1. After flipping through a magazine at the checkout counter, you realize your look really needs an update. You go home and:

a. Book a hair appointment and a manicure and pedicure! It's the fastest way to get a psychological boost.

b. Feel depressed and hopeless. You'll never lose that baby fat and see no point in shopping for new clothes. It will only make you feel worse.

c. Get over it! Your husband doesn't seem to mind, and you save time and money. Besides, those women are all airbrushed anyway!

d. Get motivated! You clear out all the outdated clothes in your closet and make a "wish list" of affordable options that you can save up for. You decide to put yourself back on the top of your priority list. No skipping hair appointments or daily workouts. You know you perform best when you feel great!

2. When Valentine's Day, birthdays, and anniversaries come around, you:

a. Already have a gift picked out. You put thought into these occasions and try your best to show your spouse that you love him.

b. Do nothing special. Your husband is not into it and never does anything for you. Why should you bother?

c. Hate the pressure and don't feel that these occasions warrant spending energy or money. Your husband knows you love him!

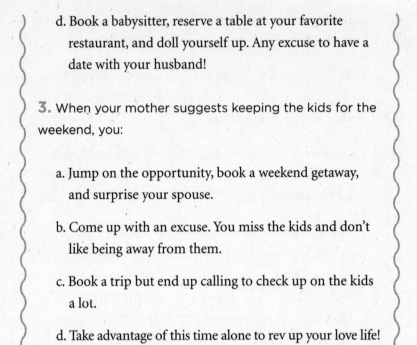

d. Book a babysitter, reserve a table at your favorite restaurant, and doll yourself up. Any excuse to have a date with your husband!

3. When your mother suggests keeping the kids for the weekend, you:

a. Jump on the opportunity, book a weekend getaway, and surprise your spouse.

b. Come up with an excuse. You miss the kids and don't like being away from them.

c. Book a trip but end up calling to check up on the kids a lot.

d. Take advantage of this time alone to rev up your love life!

If you answered mostly "a" and "d," then you are present and active in your romantic life! Your whole family is reaping the rewards of your happy and healthy love life. If you answered mostly "b" and "c," you need to reprioritize yourself and your relationship. You may be suffering from low self-esteem. Do some serious soul-searching and figure out why you are not excited about your relationship. After that, have a heart-to-heart with your partner to best figure out how you can turn things around.

Plan a Getaway—Without the Kids!

Sometimes, though, transitions and date nights are not enough to jump-start your relationship and put it back at the top of your priority list. That's when you need a vacation—without kids! Let's face it: after a while, the lack of privacy, the Matchbox cars hidden between your bedsheets, and the never-ending to-do list that any household represents just become too much. That's when you know that it's time to get away and recapture the reason you fell in love in the first place. In fact, research confirms that couples have more sex when they are on vacation. It's not hard to imagine why being out of your environment and away from the stresses of home and kids would make that the case. But here's some news: researchers have found that experiencing physical affection and sex on one day predicts a better mood and less stress the next day, which in turn predicts the same the next day. That's why vacations are so great for couples! You're free to keep the cycle going for the entire vacation!

Despite the obvious benefits, many couples never get away together, especially when the kids are little, because they feel guilty or worried. It's really too bad because, while the kids may miss you (and you *will* miss them!), they will ultimately benefit from the rejuvenation a trip can give your marriage. When looked at from that perspective, it's actually really good for the kids!

Once you've made the decision to get away, keep the purpose of your trip in mind as you plan. If your intention is to spend time together and rekindle your relationship, choose a location and itinerary that will engender that goal and provide plenty of relaxation and time to do things you can enjoy together, not separately. One friend of mine is married to a real estate developer, and every time they'd plan a getaway, she'd find herself driving around with him checking out potential real estate investments—not exactly her idea of a romantic escape. Her husband, however, was passionate about his profession and just couldn't resist a real estate guide or an enticing "for sale" sign in front of a beautiful lot. What they learned they needed to do was find a destination, say an all-inclusive resort, that minimized his wandering eye's exposure to property deals.

The same goes for cell phones, BlackBerries, and computers. If either of you has a hard time peeling yourself away from technology at home, book yourself into a B and B in the woods or an island retreat where cell phone coverage and Internet access are limited or flat-out unavailable. My good friend Jim, who runs the Spider Lake Lodge, a gorgeous 1920s lodge set in the heart of Wisconsin's Chequamegon Forest, has firsthand knowledge of what happens to people when they are suddenly disconnected from their electronic forms of communication. "On the first day, they're actually grumpy and refuse to engage fully," Jim explained. They pace the outskirts of the main room in the lodge instead of cozying up in an armchair by the fire with a glass of wine with their partner or other guests. By the next morning they're disoriented. Some people are so unaccustomed to not being "plugged in" that they actually experience symptoms of withdrawal. By the end of the second day, however, they have not only accepted the fact that they can't check e-mail or use their cell phones, but they begin to sense the freedom of it, and they realize that they actually love it! Their true personalities emerge, and they're right there enjoying the bonfire by the lake, taking out the canoe and paddles, and chatting up their hosts and the other guests. By the end, they don't want to leave!

A few years back, Sean and I planned a trip to Athens and the Greek islands. My sister and her family were living in Athens, and we planned to spend a few days with them, fly out from there to various islands, and then spend a few more days in Athens before flying home.

About three weeks before our trip, my brother Patrick heard

our itinerary and balked. "You should go to Turkey instead," he said. "Go to Istanbul and then down to Marmaris for a *gulet* boat trip on the Mediterranean." I hadn't been to Turkey since my dad was stationed in Ankara when I was in junior high. As a family, we had traveled extensively throughout this beautiful and historic country. Even as a thirteen-year-old girl, I thought Istanbul was a very romantic city, with its towering Blue Mosque, Topkapi Palace and its adjoining harem, and the Kapali Carsi covered bazaar, still as lively and bustling as it was in the fifteenth century. The *gulet* trip in Marmaris was something I had not heard of before, but as soon as I did some research, I knew it was meant to be. I could picture Sean and me on the gorgeous wooden boat, cruising the Mediterranean, eating meals alfresco courtesy of our on-board chef. The truly amazing thing was that it was so darn affordable! We'd spend more at a mediocre hotel in Minneapolis for a week. We could definitely swing it. The only obstacles were convincing Sean that it was worth the airfare-change fee and breaking the news to my sister, who I knew would be disappointed with my change of plans.

Initially, Sean was a little reluctant to incur the cost. What's so bad about the Greek islands, right? But the more we talked about the original purpose of our trip—to get away and rekindle our relationship—we knew that we needed to go to Turkey. If we were in Athens, I knew that I would want to be with my sister and especially her kids. Leah and I would get into our "sister zone," and before I knew it, I would be on a *different* vacation. It wasn't easy to break the news. She was bummed, and she let me know. When we rerouted our trip, we kept our Athens departure intact so I could at least see her for a couple of days on the way home. In Athens, exactly what I had predicted happened. Sean visited the historical sites while I hung out with my sister, shopped, and enjoyed her beautiful kids.

Sean and I will never regret our decision to change our vacation plans. Our marriage needed it! We hung out in Istanbul for five days taking in the sights, going out to restaurants, and—our favorite pastime—shopping and bargaining for rugs at the bazaar. Then we flew down the coast to Marmaris, where we boarded a *gulet* boat as gorgeous and well appointed as the description on the Web site. The food was phenomenal, and we happened to have the excellent fortune of a fun and interesting group of passengers, most of whom we still keep in touch with all these years later! Two of our fellow passengers, an adventurous Australian couple, suggested that we rent mopeds when we got to Rhodes, an island where we would lay over for a day on our way back to Athens. We did! But we rented one instead of two; I rode behind Sean, and we spent an idyllic day cruising around the whitewashed villages, stopping for an exquisite seaside lunch and an afternoon at the beach before our flight. I had never felt so young and free—like characters out of a foreign film. Quite simply, the memories (and pictures) are priceless!

Small Gestures Make a Big Difference

Date nights and vacations cannot replace the power of small, daily gestures of love: a kind word, time spent making your partner's favorite meal, or a flower for no reason at all. The true measure of a marriage is in the small things couples do for each other on a daily basis. After all, a great date or vacation really encompasses only a small fraction of the time you and your spouse spend together.

"Scheduling romance" in the form of a date or vacation is actually easier than remembering to take time out of a harried day to do something small for your loved one. On the occasions we do remember to do something that makes our spouses feel loved and appreciated, too often we end up doing what WE would like our partners to do instead of what they actually want. This is another area where communication is paramount. If you miss the spontaneous cards or other gestures from your dating days, let your spouse know. Then ask him what he would like from you. Most women assume that a spouse's answer to "What would you like?" will be more physical intimacy, but you will be surprised by his answers if you actually talk about it. One of my husband's friends complained to him that his wife never cuddles when they watch TV. When I heard the story, it really surprised me and I chastised myself for not assuming that guys are just as into cuddling. But I also wondered if he actually talked openly with his wife about it. After all it's a pretty simple request, one she could easily satisfy. Another friend of mine's husband works late regularly. Sometimes she would sit with him while he ate dinner, but other times she'd just go on with her routine of cleaning up and getting the kids ready for bed. He's an adult, right? He can take care of himself while she gets on with the evening's chores. But one evening he told her how cared for he felt when she sat and kept him company (and by implication how rejected he felt when she didn't). So now, even though some nights it's inconvenient, she always keeps him company during his dinner. Her story is a great example of the power of words and tone. He told her "he feels cared for" when she does, rather than "rejected" or "ignored" when she doesn't. He focused on results, not blame. After all, the purpose is to encourage behavior that makes us feel loved, not to guilt your partner out.

After sharing your feelings, take the high road by setting an example. Do something thoughtful for your spouse as soon as possible after your conversation. If sitting down to "talk about it" is too awkward, or you feel it will invariably be interpreted as a lecture, try something different! How about making it into a game where you both write down four things that make you feel loved and appreciated and putting these little notes in separate jars. For the next month, randomly selected one item from each other's jar each week and make it a goal to surprise your spouse with that gesture. In one month, you'll be well on your way to understanding your partner's "language of love" and reaping the relationship benefits that come from it!

Again, don't wait for your spouse to do something nice for you—lead by example. By being the partner you would want to have, you can begin to take responsibility for your relationship and build a partnership that will strengthen the entire family.

Six Small Gestures That Say "I Love You"

* A love note slipped into a briefcase or coat jacket or onto the mirror in the morning

* A favorite meal or beverage waiting when he comes home

* An unsolicited foot or neck massage

* Letting your spouse sleep in on the weekend

* A cup of coffee and the paper by his night table for when he wakes up

* A long kiss for no reason

6

DON'T GO IT ALONE!

Taking Girlfriends,

Grandparents,

and Mentors Along

for the Ride

- Girlfriends: Fill Your Bucket!

- Nurture the Grandparent Relationship

- Why We Need Mentors

- Choosing Your Mommy Mentor

- You Need More Than One

- Pay It Forward

I've come to believe there are only two things

you need in any new teaching situation to succeed—

humility and inquiry.

—LISA DELPIT

~~~~~~~~~~~~~~~~~~~~~~~~~~~~~~~~~~~~~

I love the Lisa Delpit quote above because humility is one of the most important prerequisites for motherhood. Love is our motivation, but humility allows for introspection, and that's what you need in order to parent consciously. When you parent consciously, you are open to new ideas, to change, and to doing things better. No parent is perfect. We all have room for improvement. After all, children don't come with a handbook. Since the beginning of time, parents have been making it up as they go along. However, when we admit our shortcomings (to ourselves and our children) and recognize our need to learn from others, we are better parents. Although trusting our gut is important, it is just as important to accept that we don't and won't have all the answers and to draw on the wisdom of others.

Girlfriends: Fill Your Bucket!

We all need friends, and my friend base happens to be an eclectic group with wildly different lifestyles and political points of view. Sean and I like to think it's a holdover from our *Real World* days, and we take pride in the fact that our dinner parties, like the show, bring together people who might not normally hang out for a night of sometimes heated but always fun and interesting discussions. My girlfriends are an equally diverse group: some are single, others have a spouse and kids, and still others are divorced or single parents. However, the adage "Birds of a feather flock together" helps explain why certain friends—those who are going through the very same experiences I am, *right now*—are the most comforting during this stage of my life. It's just so easy to be around them.

On a recent trip with my baby, for example, three friends offered to put us up overnight. Though all three extended heartfelt invitations, I chose my girlfriend who also happens to have an infant. Sure, her house is baby-proofed, and she had a spare crib and plenty of baby gadgets—but it was more than that. Knowing that it wouldn't matter if my baby suddenly started screaming in the middle of the night or accidently spit up on the sofa would take all the stress out of the visit. More important, though, she understands firsthand how tired a jet-lagged nursing mom can be. As a result, her expectations of me socially were, thankfully, zero! When I arrived, I changed into comfortable clothes, we ordered in my favorite takeout, and we just talked and watched TV while the two of us nursed our babies to sleep. Not exactly your typical glamorous night in Los Angeles, but it was precisely what I needed after a long plane trip. In the morning, without even asking, her husband put my stroller and infant carrier back into my rental car, and I was on my way to my appointment. It was a relaxing visit because they both get it!

If you are the mother of small children, as I am, it's just plain easier to be around people who are as sleep-deprived and frazzled as you find yourself some days. These are the friends who don't get disappointed when you have to cancel plans because your child is sick or you are simply too tired to go out. They're the ones who call to say, "I know you're sick. I'm going to the store. Do you want me to pick you up anything?" And when you tell them you're low on diapers, they show up at your door bearing not only the much-needed diapers but also *People* magazine and a box of chocolates. Like soldiers in the trenches, we look out for one another, and somehow knowing we are all in it together makes everything a little easier.

When we are in the thick of child rearing, we need women who can relate to our lives, because who else would think a day at the lake with eight kids is fun? Or think nothing of the constant little interruptions when you decide to have coffee in the presence of three toddlers? When kids are busy playing together, moms can count on time to talk, bond, and connect—even if the uninitiated might find it maddening. An additional benefit is that getting together with the kids in tow provides us a benchmark of sorts to gauge our own parenting and child's progress. That's why it's especially great for new moms to join a playgroup or meet regularly with other moms at a park or playground. I was part of a playgroup when I first moved to our town with two little ones. In a local church annex, more than thirty moms would gather for coffee while kids ranging from infants to kindergarten played in various stations stocked with toys and activities geared for their age group. I made some lifelong friends, and my kids had a wonderful, safe (and warm!) environment to run around in and meet new kids. But as a relatively new mom, I also found it extremely instructive to watch other kids interacting and even the interactions between other moms and their kids. Good and bad, these were opportunities to observe and learn from others.

We all need these mommy friends and, of course, other friends we have made over the years who are not necessarily parenting buddies; however, all friendships are not alike. In fact, some can be downright toxic. Don't hang on to friends who sap your energy. Motherhood can be draining enough without friends who drag you down. Some people have a tendency toward a negative view of life—they may expect the worst, or worry excessively, or complain constantly (even in a joking manner) about their kids or their spouse. Other friends, under the guise of being helpful, point out every flaw or second-guess every one of your decisions. Surround yourself with friends who accept you for who you are and can help you laugh at your foibles instead of wallowing in them.

Old friends in this category are a special treasure, and I am blessed to have a handful from my high school days in Arizona. Marietta, one of my best friends from high school, lives ten states away from me. Though we only talk to each other every three or four months, we always manage to pick up right where we left off. We still can't believe that we have ten kids between us, because once we get talking, it feels like we're fifteen again—laughing about our innumerable detentions, cheerleading dramas, and high school crushes. I half expect my mom to come in and tell me it's time to get off the phone! With Marietta—and with my sister and several of my other dear high school friends—it's just so easy to get to the heart of any matter or story, because with history like that, there's no need for background information or long explanations. Old friends just *know* what you're talking about. Our conversations are full of laughter and inside jokes that would leave an eavesdropper scratching his head.

I know that I am in the presence of a real girlfriend when I feel energized and uplifted after being with her. If I feel drained or anxious, I know that it is not a relationship I should expend too much energy on. Whenever I would complain about an encounter that left me more stressed out than I was beforehand, my friend Denise would say, "That person is a bucket dipper. Rachel, we need to surround ourselves with people who fill our bucket, not empty it!" When I first heard this, I bristled. It struck me as totally unchristian to seek out only those friendships and encounters that fill us. How selfish! I thought. However, the deeper I considered the matter, the more I realized Denise was right. There's a difference between an emotionally draining person and a person who is genuinely in need. A person in need is not necessarily a drain. In fact, when I serve others through volunteer work or some charitable gesture, I don't feel drained; I almost always feel great and invigorated, like I'm filling my bucket!

I once heard someone say that the difference between twenty and forty is that when you're twenty, you walk into a room and wonder if people will like you; but when you're forty, you walk into a room and wonder if you'll like them! That should be a motto for all ages! Choose your girlfriends wisely and ask yourself if this is a relationship that is supportive, honest, and authentic. Do you feel like your friend just *gets* you and that you don't have to censor your true self when you're around her? If so, this is a relationship you should nurture and enjoy more often. You deserve and need to have friendships that are liberating and rejuvenating. As for those relationships that leave you down, anxious, or even depressed, let them go! Chances are the experience is no more enjoyable for the other person. By not hanging out, you are actually doing both of you a favor—freeing up your lives to find other, more edifying friendships and experiences.

Just Say No to Bucket Dippers!
Do Your Friends Drain or Energize You?

1. When the phone rings:

   a. You can't wait to get it no matter who it is; you could use a break.

   b. You wish you had time to talk. You pick up and let whoever it is know that you will call back when you have time (and generally do).

   c. A feeling of dread overcomes you. You let it go to voice mail or the answering machine and will call back if you feel like it.

2. Your friends generally:

   a. Know you so well that they finish your sentences. They love you, warts and all.

   b. Listen while you talk and acknowledge and understand your highs and lows.

   c. Cut you off to compare whatever you are going through with their own lives or children.

3. After going to coffee with your friends:

a. You feel great and ready to tackle the day's challenges.

b. You wish you could do it all over again, because you could hang with them all day.

c. You need another coffee!

4. When you get together with friends after a long time has passed:

a. It's like no time has passed at all.

b. You get a ribbing in good fun before diving into conversation.

c. You get a lecture about being so distant that leaves you feeling unsettled.

5. When you are upset or need help:

a. You have lots of friends you could call without hesitation.

b. You have a few good friends you could call, and you know you could count on them to go out of their way.

c. You would only call your family or your spouse. Calling anyone else would make you feel strange or guilty.

If you have answered mostly "c," then you have a serious bucket-dipper issue. Moms need friends they can count on and who understand and accept them for who they are. Make it a point to surround yourself with people who lift your spirits and with whom you genuinely want to spend time. You don't need any more stress in your life!

Nurture the Grandparent Relationship

Grandparents can also be a great help to Mom (and Dad!). But their help extends far beyond babysitting. One of the most unexpected joys of parenting for me has been to witness the relationship between my children and their grandparents. Watching them interact, I see how my mother listens deeply, treating their questions and comments with the attention and respect they deserve. She is so patient with them, cutting out paper dolls or painting a little wooden train; telling them stories about her childhood, or when I was a baby, or about rescued turtles, kittens, and dogs our family nursed back to health. She intuitively knows the stories children love to hear. She remembers the excitement of getting mail as a child, so she sends them mail regularly, even if it's just stickers or a beautiful card with angels and flowers. She knows the thrill it gives little girls to open an old jewelry box filled with costume jewelry so she lets them; she saves old credit cards and Grandpa's military badges to give to my son, who lovingly stores them in little boxes in his closet. Yes, she also spoils them with clothes and toys and treats—and even a brand-new bunk bed! But it's the conversations and the small, thoughtful gestures that I know will stay with them. After all, they say elephants and grandchildren never forget.

Watching grandparents interact with their grandkids, we begin to see why the love between our children and our parents is differ-ent from our parental love and why it is something even the best parent cannot replicate. Unlike parental love, a grandparent's love for our children is not saddled with ultimate responsibility. Of course grandparents care about the well-being of their grandchil-dren, but that concern does not prevent too much whipped cream on the pancakes, a fourth or fifth cookie, or the purchase of an over-the-top toy. Grandparents also have the time (and sometimes the money) to do things parents cannot. One friend recounted how her father-in-law created a special memory for her son by picking him up from preschool early to go out for a special fourth-birthday lunch. Leaving school early and going to a restaurant in the middle of the day for some one-on-one bonding—not some-thing many busy parents can pull off. Similarly, Sean's parents once called in the middle of a weekday afternoon to take our daughter for an impromptu walk on a local pond that had frozen like a sheet of glass. Grandma, on her ice skates, walked Evita out to the middle of the pond so she could see turtles and fish swimming just below the ice. It was magical! Thanks to the thoughtfulness of my in-laws, and the fact that it didn't matter that it happened to be a Tuesday afternoon, our daughter was able to enjoy this experience before the snowfall covered it up the next day.

Children who enjoy healthy and strong relationships with their grandparents have the security of knowing that someone else in the world loves them as unconditionally and completely as their parents. Maya Angelou once said that every child deserves to have her mother's eyes light up when she walks in the room. The same applies to grandparents. When my kids go to their grandparents' houses they are made to feel like nothing in the world is more im-portant than their visit that day. Nothing! Imagine what that feels like for a child. And for parents, it is reassuring to know that there is another place that they call home should something ever happen to them. In the lives of children of divorced parents, the role of grandparents can be even more heightened, providing a sense of family history and belonging at a time when they most need it. I once heard a child psychologist say that every child should have at least two adults that they love and can turn to for sound, loving advice should they for some reason not feel comfortable talking to their parents about a particular subject or incident. I feel good knowing that my kids would go to their grandparents in such a situation.

If you are blessed with grandparents who want to be a part of your child's life, do your part to nurture the grandparent relationship—everyone will benefit. Understand that it is your job to foster this relationship. That means encouraging your children to write, e-mail, or call their grandparents. Your kids don't have to be able to type or have their own e-mail accounts to do this—you can be the scribe. Put Grandma and Grandpa's number on speed dial so they can call on their own and begin to develop a relationship independent from you.

It is your job to invite Grandpa and Grandma to be a part of your family and your child's life. If you want them around, then make them feel welcome and do not take their presence and help for granted. How can you make them feel welcome? Treat their visits with the honor and specialness they deserve. We know our own parents and what will make them feel valued. Make Grandma's favorite pie or buy Grandpa's favorite beverage. Let the calls go to the answering machine if you know it makes Grandma feel like a VIP. Here's a harder one: stay away from topics and issues that can be contentious if you know that politics and certain issues set them off. Your focus is on setting the stage so that your kids can enjoy the many wonderful benefits of a close grandparent relationship.

Don't assume they will come to events without a call or invitation. Many grandparents want to be invited, either because it makes them feel wanted or because they do not want to appear presumptuous. When you do invite them, try to be understanding of their limitations. How long is the event? Does it require sitting in uncomfortable bleachers, heat, or cold? Perhaps Grandma and Grandpa are pulled in many directions because they have so many grandkids. In this case, try to be reasonable with your expectations and help your kids to understand their limitations. Give the grandparents plenty of options, and try to invite them to activities or

Five Ways to Nurture the Grandparent Relationship

1. Recognize that it's your responsibility to foster the relationship between your kids and their grandparents.

2. Make grandparents feel welcome and special in your home.

3. Be willing to take kids to their grandparents.

4. Give grandparents and grandkids alone time to build their own relationships.

5. Accept that grandparents will indulge your kids and break some of your rules.

events that are enjoyable for them too. If Grandpa loves music, invite him to attend the school concert and skip asking him to the hockey game. While some grandparents may enjoy attending your child's events, others may instead prefer one-on-one time. In fact, the ballet recital should not be a replacement for the one-on-one time any relationship needs to grow. And if you have more than one child, consider having each one spend the night at Grandma and Grandpa's without their siblings so they can really get to know one another. It's a wonderful way for children of larger families to enjoy feeling special.

And remember, grandparents get tired. There is much truth to the cliché that grandparents love to see their kids as much as they love to pass them back to you!

Nurturing the relationship means understanding that indulging grandkids and breaking their parents' rules is one of the greatest pleasures of being a grandparent. So long as no one is hurt and the indulgence is within reason, interfering may have unintended consequences. Making Grandma or Grandpa second-guess their decisions and figure out if you would approve of a purchase or treat is a *buzz kill.* So long as you trust your parents and believe they have good intentions, let them build a relationship with your kids independent of you and your spouse.

If your children's grandparents live far away, nurturing a meaningful and rich relationship between them is a bigger challenge. My parents happen to live many states away, and we had to figure out a way for our children to bond with them despite the distance. For us, that meant letting our kids stay with Yaya and Grandpa for extended periods of time *without* us. At least once a year, we leave a few of our young children (two or three at a time so as not to wear them out!) in the care of my parents for anywhere from two to five weeks. Believe me, there have been plenty of critics. Both friends and relatives have questioned our decision to send our kids to their grandparents for such long periods of time. "Aren't you worried?" "Don't you miss them?" The answer is that no, I never worry when they are there, because I know that they are safe and loved. Do I miss them? You bet! But it's an arrangement that works for us. My kids really get to know their grandparents, and I get a much-needed break. Last year, our two oldest kids flew alone for the first time to Arizona. Sean and I were understandably nervous, but the kids were excited and seemed to have gained a lot of confidence from the experience of flying without a grown-up on their own trip to their grandparents' house.

One of the greatest benefits of these trips for my kids is that they get to see a different side of life—a slower one without a harried mom and dad trying to get too many things done in a day. They might have breakfast out on the patio or go to Starbucks for coffee, hot chocolate, and the morning paper. Some mornings they go to Mass or ride along to Home Depot with Grandpa to get the tool he needs to finally fix that leaky faucet. There's plenty of time to hang out in the children's section at Barnes and Noble or outside on the patio, where they draw, play games, and hear stories.

These stories aren't merely about day-to-day life. They are about family tradition and history, and their religious and cultural heritage, told by the most credible and natural transmitters of the information. For example, my children's faith connects them to a long line of Irish, Mexican, and Spanish Catholic ancestry. Understanding where they come from strengthens their sense of identity in this world. Moreover, recent research on the transmission of religious and cultural beliefs across generations proves that grandparents matter. Adult children whose grandparents attend church are more likely themselves to attend religious services and pass on religious traditions.

My mom can tell stories of living in Spain after the Spanish Civil War and the persecution of Catholics that ensued. This is something Sean or I could never do. Sean's parents lived through the civil rights movement and their votes for Barack Obama have a significance lost on many younger voters. Their perspective is fascinating, especially when you consider that for my kids (biracial themselves), their earliest presidential-election memories will include the campaigns of two women and an African-American! Yes, grandparents provide a window into the history and traditions of a family. But along with their insight and wisdom come other wonderful benefits for our children. Though it is very sad to see grandparents age and deal with medical problems, being around elderly grandparents who are frail or sick can teach children difficult yet important lessons about compassion and the value of human beings regardless of infirmities or disabilities—a lesson that is sadly being lost in the culture at large. These are beautiful life lessons that are best learned in the context of a healthy relationship between a family and the grandparents in their lives.

Of course, no relationship is perfect, and there are bound to be incidents that will drive you batty and make you swear, however briefly, that you'll never let the grandparents near the kids again. Like the time my mom took our daughter for a "trim," and she came back with a super-short, asymmetrical bob. I nearly popped my lid! What I found most interesting about the incident, and what actually helped me get through it, was learning that so many other moms I knew had a "helpful grandma" story to tell. My sister's mother-in-law cut off the labels and tags from the back of her son's clothes because she felt they made his back itch. This unsolicited "help" proved maddening for my sister, who passes clothes on to the next child and therefore wanted the size tags to stay on. But she summed it up perfectly when she said, "I was frustrated, but how can I stay mad when she's a remarkable grandmother?" In fact, one of the most amazing gifts that comes with the birth of a child is the opportunity for families to heal and move past old resentments or issues because the love they share for this child is greater. After all, you will be hard-pressed to find anyone else who will delight in your child as much as his grandparents. This bond has the power to overcome a great many differences of opinion!

So instead of getting upset, accept that, like with any relationship, there are bound to be problems and misunderstandings, but in all likelihood they will pale next to the benefits. It's OK to state your feelings and establish some boundaries when necessary, but keep your eyes on the prize. A strong and meaningful relationship between children and their grandparents will, in the long run, help you be a better parent to your child. It can also deepen the friendship and bonds between adult children and their parents. There simply is no substitute for the unique and deep love grandparents bring to the entire family experience.

Why We Need Mentors

In my journey as a mother, I have been blessed by the presence of experienced women who have provided wisdom and modeled diverse approaches to motherhood. These have informed and shaped my own unique style of mothering. Sometimes my "mentors" give me comfort and guidance, but mostly they mentor me by their examples. I watch, listen, and learn.

There is nothing more humbling than having kids around. Their innocence, reflected in their unfiltered thoughts and questions, is the most refreshing and wonderful part about being a parent. Once, when my seven-year-old was a toddler, he walked in on me brushing my teeth in the bathroom wearing nothing but my bra and panties and asked, "Why does your bottom jiggle when you brush your teeth?" All I could do was laugh! Jack's question came with absolutely no judgment, which is why I could never be hurt by the fact that he noticed my less-than-taut bottom. It offered a beautiful lesson about *intent*. Wouldn't it be a wonderful world if all our questions and answers came from such a loving and honest place?

In my struggles, questions, and doubts concerning motherhood, I depend on an eclectic group of loving and honest women who help bring perspective, insight, and humor to whatever issues I am dealing with in my life. Like my son, they listen to me without judgment and give me honest answers. Likewise, I try hard to listen to them without judgment and trust that, whether I follow it or not, their advice is coming from a place of love. Each and every one of them also deeply honors motherhood, especially at-home motherhood, and treats its challenges with the respect and deference it is due. Knowing that the person I am seeking advice from truly respects my work as a mom deeply affects my ability to hear and absorb their wisdom.

Choosing Your Mommy Mentor

When you are in the thick of things with kids, it can be difficult to have the perspective you need to deal with your problems. That's why you need a mommy mentor! A mommy mentor is a mom, usually older than you, whom you turn to for wisdom and insight. She's an experienced mom who's been there and can offer perspective.

Often, she anticipates what you need before you can even articulate it for yourself. She's a cheerleader who takes pride in your successes and finds it personally rewarding to support you and help you avoid some of the pitfalls she encountered. My mommy mentors are all successful moms whose children are well-adjusted teenagers and young adults. In fact, knowing her kids well is an important factor, if not a prerequisite, in my mommy-mentor selection. I am drawn to women who have raised strong families who share deep bonds. They have healthy and easy relationships with their grown children, and they truly enjoy being together as a family. Since this is my personal definition of success as a parent, I am naturally drawn to women who have achieved it. Think about it—what real estate novice wouldn't want to apprentice with Donald Trump? Who wouldn't want to learn about the computer-software business from Bill Gates? Likewise, I seek out the leaders in *my* field. Thankfully, all of them are generous and loving women who are more than willing to share their stories, including (and especially) their mistakes, so that another mom might benefit and have it a little easier.

Our neighbors Tina and Brian run the Inn at Timber Cove, one of the most quaint and charming bed-and-breakfasts in northern Wisconsin. The four-minute walk through the woods between our houses is my kids' favorite excursion. They practically beg to run errands there—bringing old magazines that I save for the guests or returning dishes from the many homemade treats Tina lovingly makes for our family. They know that when they get to Tina's there will probably be cookies just coming out of the oven, or apples to pick, or new baby kittens. There's always something, so these errands are always accompanied by strict instructions to return after fifteen minutes. Otherwise, they'd stay there all day.

Tina's teenage daughters are also my babysitters. Both are beautiful and exceptionally talented singers. However, what I most admire in them is their strong and impressive moral character; they're impervious to peer pressure. They are the kind of teenagers I hope my kids will be one day. So, needless to say, when Tina talks, I listen. I want to learn her secret. If you asked her, she'd say that there really is no secret. But I've come to realize that there is a solid philosophy behind her parenting. It's revealed in simple observations like "Some of the best conversations I've had with my girls were in the car. I think about that when I see so many young moms on their cell phones while they drive." Then I make a mental note to check my cell phone habits.

The summer before her senior year in high school, their daughter Eva had finally saved up enough babysitting money to buy an iPod. She was excited because she would be able to purchase it before the family's first-ever road trip to California. When Tina and Brian learned of Eva's plan to purchase an iPod in time for the vacation, they called a family meeting. In the meeting, they explained how they thought it would detract from the family-bonding experience in the car and during their stay in California. They preferred she save her money, but if she did buy it, there would be some rules about it on the trip. Eva naturally protested, "It's my money!" In the end, they decided to leave the decision up to their daughter. That night, Eva went to Wal-Mart, but when she got there, she decided against the purchase. I recently asked Eva, now a sophomore in college, why she didn't buy the iPod that night. "Well," she said, "when I got to the store, I began to think about the other things I could do with my hard-earned money, like have more spending money in California. Later, my experience on the trip made me realize that I would have missed out on a lot of things if I had been tuned out to the world and plugged into an iPod. To this day, I don't own an iPod. I might be the only sopho-more in college without one! I guess I just came to the realization that I don't really need one."

Tina wisely summed up the event, saying, "I was proud of Eva, not because she didn't get the iPod, but because even though she wanted it, she was open to experiencing our family trip without it." The lesson for me: don't underestimate your kids. I realized that in a similar situation, I might not have challenged my child to con-sider a technology-free family vacation. Often, in the face of peer and cultural pressure, our kids are wiser and bolder than we give them credit for.

You Need More Than One

I'm a firm believer that you should surround yourself with as many different types of mommy mentors as possible. Life hands us a variety of situations to deal with, so you need a variety of resources to draw upon. For many women, the first person to turn to is their mother. I certainly always trust my mom to give me sound ad-vice—especially when it comes to my kids. While the mother-daughter relationship can be, um, complicated, I have no doubt her deep, abiding love for her grandkids is guiding her advice, and knowing that she is coming from *that* place is important to me.

My mother has given me plenty of advice (though not always solicited!), and I don't just mean the seemingly endless and strangely appropriate Spanish sayings tailor-made for any incident or occasion you can possibly think of, like "*Mas sabe el Diablo por viejo que por Diablo*" (The devil knows more because he is old than because he's the devil)! She has given me excellent guidance in countless situations. And when the kids ask one of those questions from out of the blue that leave a parent stumped, Sean and I simply say, "I don't know. You should ask Yaya." And they do.

But even if your mom is the best possible role model, chances are that you can point to at least one thing you'd like to do differently from your parents. So find a mommy mentor who can help you. Otherwise, it is easy to fall back into old familiar family patterns you were hoping to avoid. Seek out a mentor who shares your philosophy or approach where you and your mom differ.

Hey, no one woman has all the answers! My parenting has definitely benefited from drawing on a range of women, all with different aspects of life that speak to me and that I feel are worthy of emulation. When one of my children began to experience some difficulty in learning to read, my husband and I were understandably concerned. My mother, convinced that the child was (of course!) a genius, believed that we were overreacting. "She'll catch up, you'll see," she assured us. On the other hand, my friend and mentor Carmen, a former special-education teacher, strongly encouraged us to nip the situation in the bud by taking advantage of as many special-education classes as our daughter could qualify for. "If she's on the cusp," she said, "err on the side of caution and put her in the class." We took her advice, and now our daughter is a stellar and avid reader, but to this day I'm not sure who was right, Carmen or Mom!

Like most things in life, my network of mentors was shaped by a combination of trial and error and serendipity (other than my mom, of course). Usually, I really try to get to know someone well before I add her to my mentor list. Not surprisingly, I came to this conclusion after an experience taught me the perils of a hasty judgment based on an attractive exterior picture.

Shortly after moving to my husband's hometown, we were invited to a quaint farmhouse for a cozy family dinner with some of Sean's friends. At the time, we were in our late twenties, and I was pregnant with our first child. The handsome couple was in their early forties and the parents of two beautiful teenagers. I was fascinated by the entire experience. Outside of our own families, I had never been around "married" people before in such a close and intimate setting. The hostess, now a good friend of mine, made a delicious meal complete with homemade pâté worthy of Martha Stewart's praise. The home, while modest, was warm and thoughtfully decorated; the lighting was perfect—a soft glow against the backdrop of falling snow through the windows. After dinner, we moved to the seating area near the fireplace and enjoyed wine, dessert, and great conversation. I recall my admiration for this couple, especially their warm relationship. I was totally enthralled by them. As a relatively new bride, I was captivated by the thought that I too could have a relationship like this one day! After we said our goodbyes, I looked up at Sean as we walked to the car and said, "I hope we're just like that when we're forty."

Less than one week later, we learned that our dinner hosts had filed for divorce. I was stunned! I had just declared them my marriage role models a few days earlier, and now my dream was shattered! Now, when I look at a couple or a family, I keep in mind that no picture is perfect and that no one has all the answers. It's always best to really get to know your "mentor" first and to get advice from more than one person you trust!

Pay It Forward

Sometimes instead of picking a mentor, a mentor picks you. Often, it's because she was mentored herself and wants to pay it forward,

Pearls of Wisdom:
My Favorite Advice from Other Moms

"My kids sometimes put me through hell, but I always loved them. I remember sitting up late waiting for them to come home or crying my eyes out over something they did, but I always loved them and they knew that. I think that is why they turned out great and why we all love one another so much still."   —Elfreida (mother of three, grandmother of four)

"Set the bar high, knowing in your heart that at times your kids will not meet the bar. If they know the bar is there, eventually, they will reach it, though not always in the exact time or way you imagine."

—Pilar (my mom and mother of four, grandmother of thirteen)

"Don't just stop and smell the roses; savor the sweet smells of your children. No French perfume can match the smell of a freshly bathed baby."   —Tina (mother of two)

"Your relationship with your child is like a bank account. Love and bonding moments are 'deposits'; restrictions and reprimands are 'withdrawals.' You cannot withdraw funds you do not have."   —Marisol (mother of two)

"Women have more strength than they realize. When the going gets tough, just keep going."

—Carol (mother of eleven, grandmother of thirty)

but just as often, it's because she *didn't* have a mentor and wants to be that person in a mother's life that she wishes she had had.

The influence of Sean's sister Peggy on my life and experience

"You can't have 'quality' parenting without 'quantity' parenting."
—Janie (mother of four)

"Since all children are such a precious gift and blessing from God, it is our responsibility as their mothers to teach, guide, and nourish them with love in all of our Lord's ways."
—Dar (mother of eight, grandmother of twenty-eight, and great-grandmother of sixteen)

"It's important to figure out your own life before involving someone else. If you don't know yourself, you will be constantly searching, and it will be harder to be the selfless person you need to be as a parent."
—Sharon (mother of three, grandmother of two)

"Your child develops into his own independent person, different from you. He is not always going to do what you want or expect. If you accept that, parenting your child will be a success." —Ruth (mother of one, grandmother of two)

"Don't personalize it when they pull away. That's what they are supposed to do. And remember that respect is a two-way street in the parent-child relationship."
—Peggy (mother of two)

as a mom is immeasurable. The best way to describe Peggy is that she is a ray of bright light. I'll never forget the first day I met her; she was expecting me, but was running late, so I was sitting on the couch talking with her kids, my niece, Christina, and my nephew, Erik, whom I had just met twenty minutes earlier. Suddenly the door was flung open and a gorgeous five-foot-ten-inch woman burst into the room with a brilliant smile and an unforgettable swirl of bohemian chic—long scarves, a flowing sweater jacket, dangling jewelry, lots of shopping bags, and the distinct scent of essential oils. She instantly dropped her bags, ran right up to me, and gave me a huge warm hug. At that moment I knew that I would love her forever. I also had that strange feeling that I had *known* her forever. She's insightful and fun, and she laughs big, hearty laughs that fill the room. She is also deeply committed to parenting consciously and has made it her lifework to share what she has learned.

My children adore Aunt Peggy. However, when my oldest daughter was six, she went through a phase when she acted uncharacteristically shy and distant from her aunt. Suddenly, she wouldn't hug her or thank her appropriately when given a gift or treat (of which there are many). I cringed every time I saw Evita pull away from her favorite aunt. After a visit I felt was particularly embarrassing, I called Peggy to apologize and ask her advice. "I don't know why she's being so rude. I don't want her to think it's OK to treat family like that. You're so good to her. What should I do?" Peggy instantly recognized that my reaction was about me, not Evita! "She is her own person, and she's just going through a phase," Peggy said. "I'm not hurt by it. I'm just going to love her through it! Sometimes our reactions are more about how we think something reflects on us, rather than the actual behavior of the child." And she was right on all fronts. Evita moved through the phase and has an excellent relationship with Peggy, and I was forced to look at my own reactions, and when I did, I realized that it was true—I was more concerned about how it reflected on me.

Over and over again, Peggy has taught me the wisdom of letting go and accepting and loving our children for who they are at this very moment, even if it's not exactly what we would want them to do or say. For example, instead of pushing their then twelve-year-old son, a gifted hockey player, when he seemed disenchanted with the sport, they gave him the space to let his involvement ebb and flow. Now, he is a six-foot-four professional hockey player for the St. Louis Blues—in fact, the first pick in the 2006 NHL draft (can't an aunt brag?!).

When Erik was in first grade, he took to knitting, a skill taught at his Waldorf elementary school. Even though this was not a traditional "boy" activity, Peggy, at Erik's request, hosted "knitting" playdates at the house with some of the girls from his class. Where other parents might have tried to discourage knitting playdates for a son, Peggy loved and accepted Erik for who he was—a boy who likes to knit. The story taught me a lot about not overreacting or overanalyzing my kids. They should have the freedom to be who they are, confident that their parents love them unconditionally. (In a recent interview for *USA Hockey Magazine*, Erik was asked to share something about himself that few people knew. Guess what his answer was!)

Sometimes, Peggy's advice is far simpler. On the second year in a row that my husband was out of town on Halloween, I was complaining about how difficult it was to organize four kids for a night of trick or treating. She simply said, "Enjoy it, Rachel! One day you'll ask them what they want to be this year, and they'll say, 'I'm not dressing up. Halloween's lame, Mom.'" That was all I needed to put aside my self-pity, put on my gypsy costume and take in the moment with my kids.

Peggy told me once that she wished that she had had a mommy mentor when she was raising young kids. Back then, she relied on a group of peers all going through similar experiences with their own kids. While she felt comfort in the solidarity they shared, her girlfriends lacked the perspective of an experienced mom and sometimes competition and jealousy crept in and clouded other-wise good judgment. "Now," she says, "several young moms come to me for advice. I know they value my experience, and it feels amazing to be there for someone in a way that I wish someone had been there for me." But just as important, she reminds me, "I learn from them too. I'm still parenting my adult kids and talking to younger moms helps me understand what I need to do as my rela-tionship with my kids evolves into more of a friendship."

I like to call my friend Debbie the Kool-Aid mom because I love the way her now–young adult kids have such fond memories of the things she did with and for them when they were little—baking, making crafts, and even going outside on Christmas eve when they were sleeping to put little "reindeer prints" in the snow. So fond are those memories that the kids still look forward to them, despite their age. Last year, when her teenage and college-age kids woke up on Easter and realized that for the first time, she hadn't made bas-kets for them, they were disappointed. One of them had actually been searching the house thinking Mom was hiding them extra well this year!

When I first met her, I was pregnant with my third, and Debbie (God bless her!) intuitively stepped in to fill a gap in our family program. With Sean's parents living an hour away and my parents living hundreds of miles away, she became my front line of support in town. From helping out with the kids when I was in the hospital, to inviting our oldest daughter for a day of shopping and "alone time" when she knew I couldn't get away to provide it, I know I can always count on Debbie. During the hectic month after our fourth baby was born, she'd pop in to whisk my kids away for dinner at a fast-food joint just so my husband and I could get even a one-hour break. On a particularly busy Christmas, she made me cookie dough so I could just roll, bake, and frost with the kids. She even bought me new oven mitts and cookie sheets and, having quickly discerned my cluelessness in the baking department, gave me a much-needed tutorial. Debbie's thoughtfulness is legendary in our home, but the real gift is the lesson. Debbie remembers the difficult and hectic days of parenting young kids while living far from her own parents. She knows my struggles because she's been there, and her natural response is to set out to make the life of another busy at-home mom just a little easier. What a beautiful thing to do. I've made a promise to myself to pay it forward.

7

PUT TECHNOLOGY TO WORK

Nurturing Yourself, Your Relationships, and Your Passion

- Make Technology Work for You
- Stay Connected to Family and Friends
- Just Do It! Nurture Your Passion
- Fight the Technology Demons!

*The most powerful weapon on earth is
the human soul on fire!*

—Ferdinand Foch

~~~~~~

The decision to be home with a child for a period or season of life is a weighty one that has a lot to do with how we view at-home motherhood. The trouble is that at-home motherhood's image is frozen somewhere between the dutiful and perennially cheery Carol Brady and the duplicitous and dysfunctional characters of *Desperate Housewives* (or worse, the women of Bravo's *The Real Housewives*). That's unfortunate because the actual experience has evolved in amazing ways, and explains, in some part, the appeal it has for today's young women—the most educated and successful generation of women in the history of America.

For our grandmothers and some of our mothers, staying at home was not really a choice but an expectation. Even those women with a college education and some professional experience were expected to put those interests aside to be a "good" wife and mother.

Others who were married young, with little or no professional experience, never had the opportunity to test their skills in anything other than family and motherhood. Many of these women had a yearning and restlessness. Further, without the technological advances we have today (e.g., time-saving appliances, two cars, cell phones, and the Internet), at-home moms were stuck doing household chores most of the day without time for much else. This helps explain why despite having more moms at home in the neighborhood, so many often felt lonely and short of time to enjoy the company of others and pursue personal interests.

At-home motherhood is so different now! It has been transformed by many factors, but in so many ways, the technological revolution is *the* crucial component in the evolution of at-home motherhood, giving moms time-saving tools, the freedom to nurture their passions, and often the ability to work part-time or stay connected in some way to their former work lives. Just as important, technology enables moms to explore and delve deeply into virtually any subject in the comfort of their robe and slippers.

With much of the physical drudgery eliminated by technological innovations our grandmothers only dreamed about, at-home moms have time to pursue other interests, hobbies, or passions—or simply feel better about their life because their days are more enjoyable. While many women feel that at-home motherhood is plenty (thank you very much!), others feel an emotional or financial need to include professional pursuits. For these women, technology has made it much easier to run a part-time business, participate in job-share programs, freelance, or consult—all from home. Whatever their arrangement, they know that modern at-home motherhood can accommodate their circumstances. This freedom is why modern moms know that being home does not have to be the stifling or isolating experience women once complained about. In fact, the ability to simultaneously be in both worlds—at home with your kids and contributing to your profession—can be an intoxicating feeling for moms who feel most liberated and truly creative when they are satisfying *both* essential parts of who they are.

Make Technology Work for You

I think anyone who has potty-trained a toddler would agree that the disposable diaper, invented in 1950 by a New York housewife, was the twentieth-century product that most improved the lives of mothers. Well, I say put the Internet right up there with the Pampers. You see, disposable diapers are not just about reducing the physical drudgery of diapering (no rinsing, soaking, washing); the mother who buys diapers is also buying time and, therefore, freedom. In the same way, the Internet is giving moms back time that was once needlessly wasted. Time saved is time that can be spent doing something enjoyable or rejuvenating—yoga, reading, freelance consulting or writing, painting, or playing dolls with your daughter. The accumulation of these "moments" throughout our days, weeks, and years directly affects how we perceive our experience as mothers. Make it a goal to collect these moments (as many as you can!) so you can truly enjoy your life right now so you can look back on these days with joyful nostalgia, rather than regret or disappointment for not having made the most of it.

As anyone who has ever run a home knows, the devil is in the details. The great news about being a mom today is that the Internet permits many of those details to be resolved with the stroke of a keyboard. Need to help your daughter with her research paper? It no longer requires a trip to the library; you can do it from your laptop in the kitchen. We now take it for granted, but many of us are old enough to remember having used that library relic, the card catalog. Want to ask your child's teacher about the scale of the Indian village project due on Monday? Just e-mail her. Don't know what to do with your soon-to-be-limp cabbage in the vegetable drawer? Put "cabbage" in the search engine, and in under a minute, you have a recipe, and you are on your way to putting dinner on the table. Forgot to buy your sister a birthday gift? You can have a gift-wrapped present delivered to her office by tomorrow without ever leaving your house. Moms and dads can synchronize their calendars so that Dad doesn't schedule a business meeting during the kids' school concert. If I need a pot, a bra, or a refill of my favorite night cream, I order it online, and it's delivered to my door. Many moms do their grocery shopping online. I've even eliminated the dreaded kids' shoe-shopping experience, thanks to the incredible service and shipping rates of online shoe merchants. Even the pleasurable little things in life, like catching up with the latest news, can be done at my convenience. When the baby goes to sleep, I check out my favorite online sites for current events over a cup of tea; no loud cable news show and no waiting for the nightly newscast during the witching hour, also known as the dinner rush.

No question, the Internet saves moms time and allows us to access an unprecedented volume of information, create online communities, and pursue personal interests to a degree unfathomable by at-home moms of any previous generation. And all of these advances address the problem that Betty Friedan famously exposed as the chief drawback of at-home motherhood: isolation and monotony.

Stay Connected to Family and Friends

For our mothers and grandmothers, the isolation of at-home motherhood was very real. Even though more women were stay-at-home moms, it was difficult to find time (and sometimes the money) to stay in touch with others who did not live right in the neighborhood or were not part of the school run. In addition, the list of things to do in a day didn't leave extra time for much else. For my own mother, a U.S. military wife who, for the most part, raised her family far from her native country, the cost and difficulty of staying in regular contact with her mother and sisters at times made her at-home experience terribly lonely. In those days, international calls were a luxury that the middle class didn't indulge in frequently. When they did, it was on a clunky receiver with a coiled cord that ensured you could not simultaneously attend to anything else. Not exactly convenient. Today virtually every phone is cordless, and the cell phone is a mommy essential. It not only makes us more efficient (now you can reach your husband on his drive home from work and ask him to pick up a missing ingredient for dinner), but it also gives us peace of mind. Just knowing the babysitter or the school can reach me at any time should my asthmatic son have a sudden episode is an indescribable luxury. Today, cell phones, the ease of cell- and Internet-photo transmission, Facebook, MySpace, voice-over Internet technology, video conferencing, and Twitter are changing the way we communicate with our loved ones. For the mom who is home for a large part of the day, it's a *huge* bastion against isolation.

In just the last three years, voice-over Internet protocol (VOIP) has dropped the price of international calls to my sister, who is a career diplomat living abroad, down to pennies per minute. I call my mom in Arizona and my aunts in Spain on a regular basis. Video conferencing still amazes me (remember those *Star Trek* reruns that made it seem so futuristic?). In perhaps the least scandalous use of the infamous webcam, my mother, a former Sunday school teacher, used Apple's video iChat to give weekly catechism classes to my kids who were preparing for their first communion. Of course I wish that I lived closer to my family so my kids could have those lessons at Grandma's house, but I don't, so I am grateful that technology is bridging the miles between us.

What's most exciting to me is the way the Internet is expanding our network beyond our family and friends and allowing us to meet and share ideas with mothers all over the world! Countless Web sites cover topics as general or as niche as your heart desires. Knitters, cooks, gardeners, and fans of every show, music group or celebrity can now find one another on the Web. Living in a small town or having an uncommon interest is no longer a barrier. The East Indian food fanatic in rural Wyoming, the hip urban dweller with a penchant for quilting, and social activists of any stripe can connect (and change the world!) with like-minded people around the globe.

No story better makes this point than the true story of Shannen Rossmiller, a suburban mom in Montana who is successfully fighting the war on terror from her home. This mother of three became an amateur Internet detective after watching the horror of 9/11. With her own computer and a few additional programs she has bought to enhance her tactics, she creates fake identities and chats up terrorists and terrorist sympathizers in their chat rooms. She took online classes in Arabic and uses special software to improve her translation. With the Internet, she keeps up with terrorist attacks and trolls the chat rooms in search of clues and leads. She even uses the Internet to place her pseudo-identities in specific neighborhoods, dropping the names of nearby restaurants and imams to shore up her credibility. Thanks to Shannen (who now regularly shares her information with her local FBI agency), two domestic terrorists have been arrested and convicted (one, a U.S. soldier before he was deployed to Iraq). She has also successfully helped U.S. forces find and identify terrorist cells and stopped the sale of a rogue missile. Shannen is an inspiration to all American women for obvious patriotic reasons, but is also inspiring to those of us who spend the majority of our days at home because it speaks volumes about just what can be done with an idea and a computer.

O.K., I'm not capturing terrorist enemy combatants, but I am helping to shape opinions as a blogger and writing about politics, current events, and women's issues through the eyes of an at-home mom. What truly fascinates me is how far and wide these online communities reach. I have readers from England and Eastern Europe, working moms from New Jersey and homeschool moms from Florida. Interactive Web sites bring together parents from across the globe, of all walks of life, both working and at home, to share concerns, ideas, and points of view on everything from parenting to the hottest topics of the day. And while online commentary can sometimes bring out the worst in people, it also has the ability to bring about great insight and understanding of other people's lives, cultures, and perspectives. For example, I am always amazed at how many brave men venture onto the largely female territory of Parentdish.com, a site I blog for, greatly enhancing the discussion and offering another valid way of approaching an issue.

The Parentdish community is an excellent example of the kind of networking that was once unheard-of. Mothers facing divorce, a sick child, a bullying incident, or a discipline problem can get the opinion and advice of others going through the same experience. For many women, checking in to the site is a part of their daily ritual. The connection to other women is invaluable, and real friendships develop—sometimes even moving beyond the anonymity of screen names to the real world.

Just Do It! Nurture Your Passion

Use today's technology to make space for *you*! Again, remember the preflight safety instructions discussed at the beginning of the book? Put your oxygen mask on *first*, before assisting others! What is your passion? What activity connects you to your true self? Hopefully, if you are taking advantage of modern time-saving tools, your day is at least a bit less hectic so you can engage in other activities that truly interest you.

As a mom who struggles to find that balance between my passion for my family and a passionate pursuit of my other interests, I never miss an opportunity to talk to other women in similar situations so I can learn from them.

I was recently interviewed for a feature on Celebritybabies.com. As it turned out, the journalist who came to my house to photograph and interview me was someone I'd met ten years earlier. Back then, when I was first vying for a cohost position on ABC's *The View*, Jennifer interviewed me for *Seventeen* magazine. It was great fun catching up with her and comparing notes on motherhood and everything else that had changed in our lives since we had last met. Like so many mothers these days, Jennifer has found a creative way to pursue her passion while being primarily based at home with her two kids. She is an accomplished journalist and photographer, but when she became an at-home parent, she became deeply interested in combining her love of photography with her newfound love of all things to do with the amazing miracle of pregnancy. "I love bellies!" she explained. Funny how one's life influences one's art. Her niche work with pregnant moms led to her work with Celebritybabies .com, and then to start her own celebrity parenting Web site, Celebrityparentsmag.com, dedicated to tracking and celebrating the celebrity-baby phenomenon.

Thanks to digital-camera technology, the Internet, and other advancements, the majority of her work can be accomplished from home. When she does travel, she has a wonderful and supportive husband (a crucial component!) who can pick up the slack in her absence. She's a lucky woman, who is nurturing her passion while living her dream of being an at-home parent!

Of course, it's not always possible for at-home moms to make this type of arrangement, and when they do, it's still not easy. Regardless, nurturing your passion is essential to both your soul and your work as a mom. Every mom needs to explore and discover an activity or pursuit that brings her joy—even if it's just long walks with your dogs! If, when you return from this activity, whatever it is, you feel recharged, replenished, and ready to pour yourself back into your family, then this needs to be an essential (read: **not** optional) activity in your day or week. For many women, nurturing their passion will entail some trade-offs, like a messier house or the occasional takeout on the night mom takes her class. In my case, the trade-off is sleep, because I write best when everyone is in bed and the house is quiet. On the night before my column is due, I'm bound to be up late, so I simply take it easy the next day, stay in my pj's a little longer and try (if I can) to take a catnap while the baby nurses. It's not perfect, but I am grateful for the opportunity I have had to combine my love of current events, politics, and pop culture with my voice as an advocate for at-home moms. As a blogger, I am inspired and challenged each day by the connections I have made with other moms who are as passionate about their kids and family as they are about the world we live in. I get excited when I have written something that connects with people or sparks a heated debate, because there are few subjects and discussions that cannot be enhanced by the perspective of well-informed mothers!

If the job or career you held prior to becoming an at-home mom was your passion, reflect deeply on why. What was it about your work that you really loved? More than likely, there are aspects of your job that you can still tap into or share as an at-home parent. For example, if you left a marketing job to enjoy your kids' growing-up years more fully, your training could well be employed in the service of your community or your child's school. Your education and skills are not wasted as an at-home parent! They are simply transferred from a corporation or business to your family and community. No, you won't be getting a paycheck for that, but it isn't any less significant to your family, your town, or even our country (remember Shannen?!).

As a self-described advocate and cheerleader for at-home moms, I am always noting the myriad ways that at-home moms contribute their talents and skills to their communities. Frankly, most schools, churches, and local charities would flounder without them! From school fund-raisers to food drives, at-home moms are, more often than not, spearheading the events and activities that make our world a better place. And before you write off being a homeroom mom, acting as a school-trip chaperone, and baking cupcakes for the class Valentine's party as trivial contributions, ask any teacher or first-grader—they will attest that these contributions should not be underestimated or unappreciated. Whether your passion is volunteering or baking, you should rightfully feel proud of making your corner of the world better or sweeter!

I can always recognize at first glance the Christmas cards and invitations from my friend Maria, a graphic design artist who is taking time off to raise three boys. Her talent is being lovingly lavished on recording her family's memories in scrapbooks, holiday cards, and the family Web site. "Honestly, I do it for me," she says. "I need the creative outlet, and I love that I am creating beautiful things that will help me remember this special time of my life."

If your passion is reading, painting, cycling, or gardening, your family will benefit if you *just do it*! Make time and create time. Make the nurturing of your passion a priority. Being home with your children is a lot of work, but it also has an incredible amount of flexibility. Focus on the positive: the flexibility and the fact that you are your own boss. Sure, the closets need organizing, but you have the power to decide when (and if!) they will get done. Time spent immersed in your passion, or in the pursuit of a hobby, or exploring a different side of yourself (the side that never knew she loved ballroom dancing, stamping, writing, or photography) is good for your soul and, therefore, good for your family.

If you do not know what your passion is, then you should make time to explore and try different things. Sign up for Pilates, give pottery a try, or pick up a class schedule at your local community college or university. My friend Tanya, an engineer by training, always wished that she had taken fun extracurricular classes in college, like so many of her liberal arts college friends did. Last year, she signed up for a Chinese calligraphy class on the days her youngest daughter attends preschool. "I feel so artsy!" she gushed. The truth is, between the pressure of college and then the demands of an engineering career, she never had the space to explore different sides of herself. My own sister took up flamenco dancing lessons six months after the birth of her second child, and found the stomping and physicality of the dance an unexpected stress buster, not to mention a great way to lose that extra baby weight. She returned from class sweaty and replenished, with toned biceps and calves to boot. Both Tanya and my sister are women who never really explored their creative or artistic sides prior to becoming at-home mothers, and I often wonder if something about the at-home experience (besides a flexible schedule) unleashes formerly untapped aspects of our personality. Regardless, it's safe to say that many at-home moms have the experience of discovering their true selves after becoming mothers. The key to making this discovery is to make *yourself* a priority!

Fight the Technology Demons!

If the technological trappings of modern at-home motherhood have done nothing to create free time in your days, you probably need to reprioritize. Go back and review your family mission statement (see chapter 3). Can you eliminate activities that are inconsistent with your family goals? The great thing about the new at-home motherhood is that technology should free up some time so that you can take part in activities that replenish you, in addition to those belonging to the daily grind. There is little reason these days for not having time to participate in activities that relax and recharge you (e.g., massage, your weekly lunch out with your friends) or those that truly bring meaning to you (e.g., volunteering, church on Sundays, jogging). Make time for these things by eliminating extraneous activities from your family's calendar and, of course, by making technology work for you.

That said, be careful! While moms should be enjoying the benefits of technology, we simultaneously have to battle the technology demons—you know, the temptation to be hyperefficient and constantly tuned in, thereby losing sight of the underlying purpose of our decision to be home: spending quality time with our kids. On my drive to pick up the kids from school, I hold an internal debate: should I return calls and allow my toddler to watch Strawberry Shortcake in the backseat of the minivan, or should we be singing and practicing saying colors in Spanish? And while I love (and need) time in my day to write, I recently cringed when my six-year-old complained, "Are you blogging again, Mommy?"

Today's moms are the most efficient multitaskers in the history of mothering. We pack more than twenty-four hours of work into a twenty-four-hour day! And while moms use technology primarily for "task-oriented" parenting, like helping a child with a school project or researching a symptom before calling the doctor, many of us are beginning to debate the pros and cons of being such darn efficient parents.

Case in point: parents sending kids off to college for the first time are increasingly tethered by text messaging. My sister-in-law is grateful for how it enables her to stay connected and close with her daughter, who is going to school out of state. But another friend of mine has a no-texting rule with her out-of-state daughters, fearing that constant texting is altering this rite of separation. She wants her girls to try to figure things out for themselves (as she did in her college years), instead of reflexively texting Mom when a problem arises.

Yet, I remember what a hassle it was for my mom to coordinate rides and after-school activities with multiple teenagers. Text messaging would have cut down on the times my sister and I were left waiting for my mom to pick us up because cheering practice or our game ended early and there was no way to reach her because she wasn't home. I feel downright ancient even telling this story!

Think honestly about the use of the cell phone, television, computer, or BlackBerry in your house. Is technology helping you to spend more or less time with yourself or your family? If you suspect there is a problem, the best thing to do is to remove it from your life for a period of time. The television is my little demon. As a self-professed news junkie, I am always trying to find the appropriate balance between being informed and using the television as a constant background noise. When I feel that the television is starting to take over, I take it out of my life completely for three or four days. By the end of my self-imposed restriction, I find that I rather like the silence, and I turn the television on much more infrequently. What's most interesting to me is that my usage ebbs and flows, and I know that it requires periodic moderation and self-adjustment.

When it comes to technology, the debate and calls for balance rage on, but I will always marvel that my husband can call me on his cell phone from the video store and read off movie titles while I look up reviews on the Net. We can decide together and avoid disappointment later. Now *that's* technology working for families!

Are You Nurturing Your Passion?

1. At a recent party at your house, your husband's boss notices a painting you made years ago when you were studying art in Paris and asks you who the artist is. You:

a. Sheepishly own up to your work and quickly change the subject. He probably knows it's you and is just trying to be polite.

b. Confidently inform him that he's looking at the artist. Then you pull out your portfolio and engage him in a conversation about art and your studies in Europe. Who knows? He may commission a painting for his new digs.

c. Don't answer the question and ask him if he needs a refill on his brandy Manhattan. Discussing your former life as an artist is too painful.

2. Your sorority sisters are begging you to join Facebook. You:

a. Join, but don't actively participate. You feel guilty when you decline others' online invitations.

b. Join on the spot and start searching for your long-lost seventh-grade pen pal from Sweden.

c. Refuse to join! You don't understand all the fuss about social networking. Sure you miss your old friends, but who has time for old friends once kids come along?

3. Your living room is piled high with old *Architectural Digest* magazines. You just found out that a local college is offering an online course. You:

a. Register for the class, but remain apprehensive about what you can really get out of an online course.

b. Can't believe your fortune! All the fun of learning without the stressful college pressure to make the grade. You don't know what to expect, and you're not even sure if you'll be good at it, but that's not going to stop you from giving it a try!

c. Tell yourself you're too old to revive that dream. Besides, your husband will complain about the cost and time away from the family.

4. You run into your old creative-writing professor, who reminds you of your natural talent. You:

a. Go home and finally join your town's creative-writing club.

b. Get inspired and that very night, surf the Internet into the wee hours. Once you find the perfect site for you, you have every intention of lobbying them for a blogger position.

c. Tell him that your window has closed—for now. Maybe after the kids go to college you'll finally sit down and write that novel that's been simmering in your head since grad school.

If you answered "c" for any of these questions you are not making the most of technology to nurture your soul and your passions. You need to reprioritize your life and take advantage of the flexibility that at-home motherhood offers. If you answered mostly "a" for these questions, you are on your way to finding a perfect balance between your love for your family and that activity that feeds your soul. If you answered "b" for any of these questions, you have the right attitude! In fact, you are probably already involved in your passion. Your spirit is an inspiration to your kids and to other moms!

8

ACE YOUR SPACE

Creating a Soulful Home

- Start with the Family Table

- Your Home Should Encourage Togetherness

- Get the Most from Your Space

- The Outside Matters Too

- Little Things Mean a Lot

- Home as Sanctuary

To be happy at home is the ultimate result of all
ambition, the end to which every enterprise
and labor tends, and of which every desire
prompts the prosecution.

—SAMUEL JOHNSON

~~~~~~~~~~~~~~~~~~~~~~~~~

spend a great deal of my time inside my home, especially in the winter. Winter in northern Wisconsin is as cold as it is beautiful, and my favorite way to enjoy it is from an armchair by the fire in my cozy, warm living room (remember, I'm from Arizona!). From my armchair, I can look out at the huge snow-covered pine trees out back and the wildlife that will inevitably pass by if I sit for more than ten minutes; it is a scene so eerily similar to the place where Lucy met the faun in *Narnia* that the kids and I have often talked about installing a lamppost out back just for fun. Though I spend a lot more time outside in the spring and summer, for the most part, my work as a mom—cooking, cleaning, and caring for my children—is inside work. That's why I have worked hard to ace my space! My goal: to create a home that is functional (less work for me) and an environment that reflects our values.

A few years ago, we knew we needed a bigger house. We had three kids, and I was pregnant with our fourth. We were bursting at the seams, and I was ecstatic about leaving behind what was quite possibly the most dysfunctional kitchen I had ever been in (scarce countertops, no dishwasher, and a stove that was nowhere near the sink!). We spent more than two years hunting for the right house. Of course, we were juggling many considerations, including our budget. Thankfully, the one thing we did agree on was that after living in a house that had outgrown our needs and turned cooking, something I actually enjoyed, into drudgery, the new house needed to be a place that worked for me—the at-home parent who was home with kids for most of the day! With that consideration at the top of our list, we finally found a two-story, five-bedroom home with five acres of woods. It's not the perfect place, but I fell in love with it. We had to renovate quite a bit, and my bathroom is still the size of a small closet. The house definitely needs some re-siding too! But the land surrounding our home is beautiful, and the views from my kitchen and virtually every other room in the house connect me to nature and the dramatic changes of the seasons for which the Northwoods of Wisconsin are known. I knew we could make this house a charming and functional home worthy of the important work that goes on inside of it.

Start with the Family Table

We all want a house that is warm and functional; however, if you are an at-home parent, your entire day depends on it. So, how do you start? I say, start with the family table! Why? Because family meals are central to the soul of your home life. Regularly eating together anchors your family and provides many more benefits than most of us think about. It's not hard to imagine that children and teens who share meals regularly with their parents have better overall diets and finer table manners, but did you know that they are also more likely to have bigger vocabularies and better grades, and are less likely to smoke, drink, have sex, get depressed, consider suicide, or have an eating disorder? No wonder more and more families are recognizing what was lost when our culture down-graded the significance of the family meal and eschewed the warmth, smells, and comfort of home cooking for the convenience of takeout and processed, microwavable fare. Today, there is a promising uptick in the return to the traditional sit-down, no-TV, and no-phone-calls family meal. Parents are discovering that the more regularly they have them, the more enjoyable they are! That's right: family meals take practice, and those families who have them infrequently actually report bad experiences when they finally wrangle everyone around the table. The fruits of family meals (and all those big teenage payoffs) come when it is a daily event every-one can count on.

Giving thought and importance to our family table and meals can be the difference between a house and a home; between people who happen to live together and a family who is building mean-ingful bonds and a family identity. One of the saddest things I ever heard a child say is, "We don't have a culture." In my estima-tion, this child wasn't referring to an ethnic or cultural deficit. It was the dearth of conversations: the kind of family stories, legends, and information shared over dinner through which cultural, po-litical, and religious values are learned. In that context, the family table is a sacred place where families literally and figuratively "break bread."

That's why, when we began renovations on our house, we spent the most time and money on our kitchen and, specifically, the design and location of our table. We decided on an island stove so I could look out at the family as I cooked. In addition, we decided that the center island would also serve as our family table. However, in order to retain the feel of a traditional table we worked with our kitchen designer to invert the way stoves are normally incorporated into islands. We did not want counter-height chairs, which can be dangerous for small children and make you feel like you're eating at a bar. Instead, our *stove* is counter height, and the surrounding sides drop down to table height. We sit on normal dining chairs, and I'm still facing the family when I have to stir a pot or dole out seconds.

Like so many moms, I spend a great deal of time in the kitchen, and it was important to me not to feel cut off from the family action. Now our kid-friendly kitchen island serves so many other purposes in addition to eating. It's a place for kids to do homework, frost cookies, or simply hang out while I cook.

Thanks to our remodeling, we were able to really reflect on the importance of our family table and incorporate our values and needs into our kitchen design. But you do not have to move or renovate to get the desired effect. Take a hard look at your own family table. Is it a place where everyone is comfortable? Is your table the right size and shape? Some people just love round tables and feel that they are more conducive for conversation. However, if yours is a smaller family, you might feel that you fit better around a square or rectangular table. What about the chairs? Are they comfortable for everyone, including your small children? If these questions make you want to go out and get a new table, it doesn't necessarily have to be new! Once you decide on the shape and size, you will find plenty of options at thrift stores or even garage sales. So long as the table is sturdy, and you like the legs, a beautiful tablecloth can hide a multitude of sins. The important thing is to think about your family and perhaps even talk to them about what they like so that it can be a place where everyone enjoys being together—not just for eating, but for other activities as well.

Often, we can get a little too hung up on how things look. I love interior design and strive to make my space as beautiful as possible, but with a busy and growing family, sometimes aesthetics just have to take a backseat. When I had my fifth baby, I found myself leaving the kitchen all the time to nurse in my comfortable living room armchair. I wanted to be in on the action, in the kitchen, where the rest of the family was, but I just couldn't get comfortable enough to nurse in our kitchen chairs. After a while I thought, "What the heck am I doing??" and I moved my armchair right into the kitchen. Martha Stewart probably wouldn't approve of the way it stands out in the room, but as long as I'm nursing our baby girl, it's staying!

Your Home Should Encourage Togetherness

After the kitchen, the most important gathering spot in your home is going to be the living or family room. Remember when houses had a "guest living room" that no one was allowed to enter? When company came, even the owners of the house felt uncomfortable in these showrooms, which, frankly, never made for a warm and relaxing visit. Thankfully, people are far more practical and casual

Rules to Make Your Table a Family Table

1. Starting with a prayer or thanksgiving ritual sets the tone.

2. No distractions! Turn the TV off; let the phone ring. Make this hour sacred.

3. Get the kids in on the food preparations—they are more likely to eat their food if they help.

4. Keep dinner conversations enjoyable by avoiding topics like "You never clean your room, take out the trash," etc. This is not the time to nag.

5. Manners matter. This is an opportunity to teach kids important lifelong skills.

6. Keep the conversation inclusive. Allow every member to contribute. Don't let one person take over the conversation.

7. Keep it respectful—no laughing at others or teasing allowed.

8. Forget about the "no politics and religion" rule! This is a time for families to discuss the world around them and to share and instill your family's values. At the same time, allow your kids to have different opinions and to share them without criticism.

about entertaining now and know better than to waste valuable space and money on an "off-limits" room. So forget the plastic slipcovers and china display cabinets and create an atmosphere in your home where the kids are welcome everywhere. Of course, that doesn't mean the kids don't have to be respectful of their environment and take care of things, but one of our goals was to make the living room a place where everyone would want to hang out instead of their bedrooms. The centerpiece is the fireplace, which is surrounded by the couch and a couple of comfortable armchairs spacious enough for kids and grown-ups to sit in together. Our living room is connected to our kitchen, and this is where we read, gather for family meetings and prayer, and entertain. Ours is a great room, and we love that our guests can wander between our living room and kitchen. I like that I never feel left out of whatever is happening while I'm making dinner or refilling a friend's cocktail.

While we have a small TV in the kitchen, we made a conscious decision not to have a television in the living room. This room is

To make reading extra special during holidays or the various seasons of the year, I keep "out-of-season" books out of circulation. For example, I bring out all the Christmas books at the beginning of December when I take out the Christmas decorations. Then I keep them in a basket in the living room so that we can read and remember them during the holidays. After the holidays, I store them away in separate, marked plastic containers in the basement (you can do the same with movies!). Saving them for a special time makes the books seem new again, and by not having them scattered or lost somewhere in the bookcase, we end up reading these special books regularly during the season!

reserved for conversation and plenty of reading by the fire. Although the kids' bookcases are in their own rooms, their books are just as likely to be hanging out on the couch or side tables in the living room. Creating an environment that encourages reading also encourages togetherness. Most nights, I read my kids their bedtime stories in the living room, where we can all snuggle up and they learn to associate reading with a positive cozy experience.

Our living room also includes a small family altar, where we keep religious symbols, candles, and prayer books. Our children help to change the altar cloth and various statues to reflect the seasons of our liturgical year. During Lent and Advent, we gather around it nightly to light candles and pray. Your faith may or may not use shrines and altars at home. But you can certainly create other tangible symbols of what you share together as a family, such as cherished photos and mementos of trips and special occasions. Don't forget to include photos of grandparents and great-grandparents; old family photos remind the children of their ancestors, heritage, and culture. Creating a designated space that helps your family understand its identity and values brings history and meaning to your family gatherings.

Get the Most from Your Space

Sadly, running a home involves some degree of drudgery. You can't escape it, even if you are fortunate enough to have hired help. And chances are that there is at least one chore you despise, but *have* to do. For me, the chore is laundry. Yes, I've heard of those people (my sister included) who like doing laundry and even find it to be soothing and calming. For me, it's pure tedium . . . and with seven people in the family, it's also never-ending! In our previous house, my washer and dryer were in the basement—which compounded my dread and resulted in piles of laundry accumulating to seemingly insurmountable heights. When we bought our current house, the washer and dryer were on the first floor. "Wow," I thought, "what an improvement!" But then I saw a friend's second-floor laundry room and had an incredible "A-ha!" moment. Of course! Other than kitchen towels, everything you put away is on the bedroom level. Thankfully, it wasn't too late when we discovered we had plumbing for a laundry upstairs! I still consider my upstairs laundry one of the best decisions we *ever* made in our home. It has cut down on so much work and needless trudging up and down the stairs.

The point here is that anything you can do to save time on housework in your home is time you can spend doing other, more enjoyable activities—like hanging out with your kids! One of my friends loves to ski with her family on the weekend, but dreaded the mess and cleanup when everyone came home. So, she designed a mudroom with coat hooks, benches, and plenty of storage, and she had it built into her garage. That way everyone's wet jackets and equipment stayed out of the house.

Think about the chores you least like and what you could do to minimize or make that job a little less dreadful. It can be as simple as a big plastic container in the garage so even your toddler can help put away yard toys or building cubbies into the closet for easy backpack storage after school. Creating function doesn't necessarily have to cost a lot of money. However, if living without a dishwasher, as I did for several years in our former house, is driving you nuts and making you feel like Cinderella (*before* she slipped into the lost glass slipper), then you need to prioritize your budget to meet that need. Surely, with some creativity (and patience), you can find a way to fit that time-saving appliance or renovation into your budget. After all, it is an expense that can have a profound impact on how you experience your days as an at-home mom—a priceless investment!

Our laundry room ended up in an upstairs room we call the "rec room." The rec room is a TV room with a built-in desk, where the kids draw and do projects or homework. It's also where we keep our workout equipment—an elliptical machine, a spinning bike, and a Total Gym. This multipurpose room has been a godsend for so many reasons. For one, I can work out, watch kids, run the laundry, and see my favorite show all at the same time! It's also a place the kids can retreat to when we have guests. When we're ready for some kid-free conversation, we'll make them popcorn (Grandma and Grandpa recently bought the kids an old-fashioned popcorn machine for the room), pop in a movie, and get some much-needed adult time. In December, the kids are in charge of decorating the rec room. They have their own prelit artificial "kids" Christmas tree with nonbreakable ornaments and decorations so they can have at it! Now I don't feel bad when I don't let them handle the delicate ornaments on the big tree downstairs.

Even if you don't have a family room or rec room, consolidating activities into one room allows you to eke out together time while you take care of necessary chores. Maybe you have a basement that is waiting to be put to use. If your washer and dryer are down there, how about adding exercise equipment so you can sweat between loads? What about a TV or a play space for the kids so you don't have to be separated from them while the laundry is going? Or a desk or computer so you can accomplish a few other tasks too? Just as important, try to create a space that kids can happily retreat to when grown-ups need some alone time. They need it as much as you do!

The Outside Matters Too

Don't forget the outdoors when it comes to your home. One of the first things Sean did when we moved into our new home was to find the perfect place for a campfire. He dug a pit and put chairs around it—including little kid-sized ones he makes out of old logs (a skill he learned during his days as a lumberjack performer). Our campfire is a place for us to hang out and make s'mores during the short, sweet summer months in Wisconsin. Maybe your family's gathering place is a portable, store-bought fireplace on your patio, or maybe it's the swing on your front porch. Whatever it is, don't forget the outdoors when it comes to creating spaces for your family to gather and relax.

This may sound a little exotic to a lot of you, but our kids like to logroll and they even compete in the logrolling world championships every summer. Up until last year, they attended logrolling school in Hayward, Wisconsin, about an hour away from our town. As our family grew and gas prices increased, we decided to create a place for them to logroll right in the backyard. Sean traded a used boat motor for an old wooden tank owned by his former boss at Scheer's Lumberjack Show. Now that old wooden tank sits in our backyard, and the kids get their logrolling lessons from their dad after he comes home from work. I'm happy that I don't have to drive an hour for their lessons, and the kids would rather learn from Dad anyway. OK, I know that logrolling isn't the most popular or convenient sport for your kids to take up, but there are plenty of other, more practical things you can put in your backyard, front yard, or driveway to generate the same bonding experience. A basketball hoop? A soccer goal? Tetherball? A trampoline or a swing set? The point is that you should find ways to make the outdoors just as inviting a place to be together as indoors so you can enjoy fresh air and family bonding at the same time!

Little Things Mean a Lot

Every home has its own style and rhythm because every mother and her family are so very different. One of the greatest pleasures of being a mom is creating a warm and inviting place for everyone to come home to. Yeah, I know it's old-fashioned to say so, but except for a few rare exceptions, it's pretty much up to moms to do it. And we don't just set the scene. We set the tone. It's up to us to make the home a sanctuary as opposed to a source of friction or stress. For me, this has been an unexpected joy of motherhood. I take pride in knowing that our home is my family's favorite place to be; that when they are away, they look forward to coming through these doors. The smell of a home-cooked meal, a roaring fireplace, a warmly lit room, a tidy, albeit lived-in, house—these are touches that affect our senses and create an indelible memory of family life.

I know my family appreciates how hard I work to create a warm environment, and that's never been clearer to me than during the process of writing this book, when I have had to pare back my usual activities around the house to make time for writing. When suddenly presented with a dinner of chicken nuggets versus a steaming, homemade pot of chicken-dumpling soup, my family takes notice! The kids have lodged plenty of complaints, especially the older ones, who are more critical of the way Daddy does things ("Fishsticks again?!"; "Dad just doesn't do the voices in Nancy Drew the way you do, Mom!"). We even had to have a family meeting to address their concerns. We told them to buck up, because families need to work together and support one another's endeavors. Soon, I reassured them, things would settle down and go back to normal. I have loved working on this book project, and the time that I have spent working on it has been good for me, but I also realize that it has been good for them too. My whole family has gained a renewed appreciation for everything I do—and so have I! On the days I have office hours, they miss my cooking, but they also miss my availability to show me their rock collections, lie in bed and talk before bedtime, or snuggle up for a Friday night movie. Truthfully, it has been nice to be so missed and reminded of my indispensability.

As a mom, I want my home to reflect what I value most: my family. That's why I love to have plenty of family photos around, and I frame my kids' artwork and hang it with pride in our kitchen and living room. My daughter Evita is quite a good artist, and a collection of some of her best art is on display in the living room. She was so proud when we framed her work and put it in such a place of prominence. Now, when guests visit, it is a wonderful conversation piece that she can speak about. Maybe you too have family photos or artwork to display?

I prefer when the house is organized, tidy, and beautiful because I am deeply affected by my surroundings. Whether it's a fine piece of furniture, an orchid in a vase, or a handful of daisies cut by my daughter in the garden, my environment affects my mood, and I want to be in a house that lifts my spirits and reflects my passions. Over the past few years, as my blogging and writing have picked up, I have taken over our family office. The more time I spend there, the more it has become "my" place. I've come to realize that I *need* a place just for me, where I can get away to think and write. Right now, though, it isn't at all how I'd like it. I hate the wood paneling, and my desk is too big and cumbersome. Frankly, the whole room, including the furnishings, lacks a feminine touch that would make it "mine." So, next on my list (after the book!) is to paint and redecorate the office. In the meantime, I have purchased a good lamp and put up a few family pictures on the desk for inspiration. My walls, however, are covered with Scotch-taped paintings and drawings from my kids, who periodically bring them in as tokens of encouragement for my project. Those will stay, however I decorate!

Home as Sanctuary

Remember the old adage "Show me your checkbook and I'll tell you your values"? Your home is a sanctuary from the outside world and the place in which the most important things in life unfold. Creating your family's "sanctuary" is an important task that requires thought and love.

In Catholic theology the home is actually called "the domestic church." I love the term because it gives the home the spiritual importance and dimension it deserves. It sends a message to the family and to the outside world that it is a place of great consequence, a school of love.

Giving my home and the "business" that goes on inside of it the deference it deserves has had a tremendous impact on the way I view my work as an at-home mom and the way my family has come to appreciate what I do to make a warm and loving home. How many of us have told a child to pick up his mess with the age-old command "Because I said so!"? I know I have! But I've also learned from experience that my kids are less resistant on the days when I have the patience to explain that picking up our mess is more than a chore; it's a way to show respect for our home and what we do to make it nice and cozy for them. I know my kids appreciate it when everything is clean and orderly, because when it's not, they're more agitated; they'll even complain that the house is a mess! On those days, I know that experiencing the discomfiting feelings of a messy home for a day (or two!) is good for them and will help them appreciate when it is not.

Creating a home that feels like a sanctuary from the outside world is especially important for family members who have to spend hours away from it at work or school. To reinforce this sense of sanctuary, we have a holy-water font by the front door. It was a gift from my mother-in-law, Carol, who bought it for me on a trip she took to Italy. It's made of beautiful blue-and-gold mosaic tiles, and knowing the trouble she went to to find one she knew I would love has made it all the more special to me. As we leave and enter, the act of blessing oneself is a physical reminder to our family that this is, indeed, a sacred place—even if it is occasionally very chaotic. For the same reason, you will often see a mezuzah, a small scroll containing biblical passages and prayer, affixed to the doorpost of a Jewish home. In a literal sense it's there as a reminder of God's commandments and protection, but it also serves as a reminder to reflect on and appreciate the difference between the outside world of bustle and commerce and the domestic sphere of home and family.

A tradition we follow in our family is performing a ritual blessing of our home every year on the Feast of the Epiphany. Epiphany (or Three Kings' Day) is when Christians celebrate the day the Three Wise Men brought gifts to the baby Jesus in Bethlehem, and in Spanish cultures, it is a holiday that rivals Christmas. After dinner, we open our front door, and with chalk, my husband inscribes the numerals of the current year and the initials of the wise men at the top of the door. Then, we cut a branch from our Christmas tree to dip into a jar of holy water to bless each room of the house. Many other religions also have blessings and rituals to sanctify the home.

Though our family uses religious blessings, other things you can do celebrate the idea that your family home is a very special place. Call a family meeting. Grab pens and some paper, and ask everyone to write down his or her ideas about why the house is special. Reasons might be as concrete as the beauty of its French doors or as intangible as liking the way it creaks when the wind is howling. Then weave the reasons together to create an ode to your home. Read it out loud, with perhaps everyone reading some lines. Then pick a time when you will read it regularly, whether once a month or every New Year's Eve or whatever feels right to you to reinforce the significance of your home.

When weighing the decision to buy our current house, both the cost and the hundreds of little decisions surrounding our renovations prior to moving in, I often contemplated a story about Mother Teresa and her Sisters of Charity home in the heart of Guatemala City. City planners informed the sisters that they were using valuable land and that they would have to move so the land could be put to better economic use. The city's intention was to level the building where the sisters lived and served the poor and to build a market on the site. When Mother Teresa heard about this she simply said, "We are a market too—a more important market. We are selling love." That simple and profound statement had a powerful impact. The government officials not only permitted the sisters to stay but even threw in some extra land!

At its core, a family is also in the business of love, and the home is the place where this "business" unfolds. Mother Teresa's story makes a strong case for giving the home its place of honor. The lessons in love taught in the home have a greater impact on the world than the things that happen in places of commerce or government. Indeed, those institutions are just that—institutions. It is the people who inhabit those institutions—their character, honesty and the passion that they bring to their work—that can make those agencies forces of good in our world. These virtues are first—and best—learned in the family home, where members learn to love, share, and care for one another.

Am I Creating a Soulful Home?
Is My Home a Sanctuary?

1. When I think of my home, the word that comes to mind is:

    a. Love.

    b. Warmth.

    c. Chaos.

    d. Fun.

2. On a typical evening after the kids go to bed you will find me:

    a. Reading in my favorite chair. I love the quiet.

    b. Fast asleep. I'm exhausted.

c. Alone, watching mind-numbing TV to forget about the laundry and housework that's piling up.

d. Hanging out with my hubby, talking and watching our favorite show.

3. When I reflect on my day in the evening, I feel:

a. Proud of what I accomplished.

b. Tired, but grateful.

c. Resentful. I'm tired of being tired.

d. Happy to be alive!

4. On a scale of one to 1 to 4, I would rate my home's function and beauty as:

a. (4) I've worked hard and found clever ways to make my house organized and charming.

b. (2) I wish my spouse and I agreed on the importance of aesthetics in a home so we would follow through with more of the changes I think it needs.

c. (1) I hate my house, and that's why I don't like having company.

d. (3) It's not perfect, but I'm making improvements and have a long-term plan.

If you answered mostly "a," "b" and "d," then your home is your sanctuary or it is on its way to becoming the place you want it to be for you and your family. If you answered mostly "c," you need to consider the psychological and family benefits of a home that meets your family's needs and makes your day easier. You are home most of the day and deserve a space that works for you and makes you proud.

9

20 MOM MUST-HAVES

Setting Yourself Up for Success

This is the most important journey of your life, and hopefully, this book has inspired you to appreciate more fully the magnitude and consequence of what you do every day for your children, your family, and the world at large. It is in that spirit that I offer my list of mommy must-haves: a list full of items that make my life easier, more organized, and, yes, more beautiful. While some will surely balk at a list of must-haves for at-home moms that includes spa products, I say modern at-home motherhood is a demanding and dynamic lifestyle, and we need more than a playpen and a TV. Items that save us time, encourage us to take excellent care of ourselves, and replenish our spirits are must-haves. Our goal isn't to survive motherhood, but to find pleasure and meaning in it. So banish the guilt and set yourself up for success!

1. The Right Diaper Bag

What mom couldn't use the convenience of a large bag designed to help you keep things organized? That's why I am a huge fan of *purse* diaper bags—whether you have an infant or not! Purse diaper bags look exactly like the high-end handbags you love, except that they have plenty of compartments and features for organizing the many items moms carry around on a daily basis: not just makeup and a cell phone, but sippy cups, bags of snacks, toys, hand sanitizer, crayons, pacifiers, wipes, an extra outfit for your baby, or a sweater for your toddler. Purse diaper bags have plenty of clever compartments and easy-access pockets, and they're made of durable, wipeable material on the inside that can withstand spills and any other accident. My favorite site for a large selection of stylish purse diaper bags is www.diaperbagboutique.com because they have a range of price points to choose from. If you can afford to splurge on this one, go for it! Choose a classic beauty and you can use it indefinitely. My favorite high-end line is Mia Bossi. For mid-priced bags I think Nest is the way to go. You'll get all the impact for under two hundred dollars. If you are looking for all the features without the price, then Skip Hop is your brand. Most of their bags are well under one hundred dollars. For a great overnight diaper bag that can do double duty as your own weekend getaway bag, check out the line by OiOi. Their overnight diaper bags are chic and durable and way too cute not to take on your next trip sans baby. Here's the bottom line. It wasn't very long ago that diaper bags were made of cheap vinyl and plastered with pictures of Winnie-the-Pooh. Thank goodness today's moms have so many cool and dignified options. No one wants a diaper bag that looks like a diaper bag, right? Yet many of the features in diaper bags are useful for moms beyond the diaper years. So, invest in a purse diaper bag you love—one that has the look and quality of a high-end handbag—and you'll get years of use out of it!

2. Magic Eraser

Magic Eraser is a sponge by the Mr. Clean product line. This sponge gets out virtually any stain your child can put on the walls, furniture, or countertops. I love it because it allows me to keep my cool when I catch my toddler drawing on the wall. It even took permanent marker off my dry-erase board in the kitchen. It's that rare product that actually lives up to its claim—it magically removes stains that you thought were impossible or nearly impossible to remove. The incredible efficacy of the Magic Eraser spawned a series of online rumors claiming that it contained formaldehyde. It doesn't! But look, I wouldn't use it as a teething toy for the baby— it's a cleaning product, so keep it where you keep all your cleaning supplies: away from kids! It's a useful product that can save you time and tears.

3. Boppy

If you nurse, as I do, you deserve to purchase items that make your nursing experience comfortable and enjoyable. After all, the easier it is for you, the longer you will be able to give your baby all the wonderful benefits of breast milk. My favorite item is the Boppy pillow. The Boppy is so popular that it's on most new moms' must-have lists, but what many first-time moms don't realize is that the Boppy is one of the few baby products you can use long after the infant stage. When my kids are sick and congested, for example, I use a Boppy for a pillow to help them sleep comfortably in a propped-up position during the night. The kids also use it as a pillow when they watch television on my bed or on the floor, and it's the perfect laptop pillow for when I write in bed. With each child, I purchased a new cover (you can find them online). The latest is my favorite, a chocolate brown chenille . . . sooooo soft! The pillow is the same one I purchased ten years ago, but the cover makes me feel like baby number five finally got something new!

4. Hooter Hider

A hooter hider is a clever biblike cloth that you can strap around your neck for instant discretion while you're nursing. These little pieces of cloth have ignited firestorms of debate on mommy blogs because some nursing enthusiasts think that it perpetuates the idea that nursing is a shameful thing that should be hidden. While I respect anyone whose goal is to normalize breast-feeding, for me it's had quite the opposite effect. I'm a much more confident public nurser thanks to hooter hiders. Unlike a blanket that can make a baby feel smothered or fall off as Mom tries to peek in to help baby latch, hooter hiders allow for Mom and baby to see each other while keeping *other* eyes out. I love the line by Bébé au Lait because they have so many wonderful fabrics to choose from. My only regret is that I did not learn about it sooner! My dear friend Cat purchased several for me when I had my fifth baby. I couldn't believe I had suffered without it for so long. Now it's *my* favorite baby shower gift. It may not pack a huge "Wow!" at the party, but I know the mom will be thinking of me for months to come because she will never want to leave home without it.

5. Notebook/Journal

A notebook or journal designated for writing down those precious moments is a mommy must-have. The good news is that nothing fancy is needed. A leather-bound journal is nice, but even a spiral notebook will do. No more guilt about not writing that stuff down. Keep one in the kitchen, the living room, and the bedroom so there's always one close by when your daughter says, "Kissing is 'usgusting!!!" A wide-ruled spiral is a good idea if you plan to let the kids write things down too. You may even want to tie a pen or pencil on a string to the notebook so they are always together. The point here is to make writing down these moments easy and painless so you actually do it. Many years passed before I figured out this little trick. True, I lost a few years, but happily there are many more to come!

6. Home Spa Products

I love to go to the spa! It's a quiet like none other: silence interrupted only by the sound of trickling water from a Zen fountain in the lobby and a soothing Enya sound track over the speaker system. When people speak to you at the spa, it's always softly and to see if there is something they can do for *you*. No wonder moms fantasize about living in a spa! The problem is that it's not always easy to afford the time and money to go. While there's no substitute for an authentic spa experience, you can pamper yourself at home more often and for less money by purchasing high-quality home spa products. With some clever items at home, sending Dad and the kids to the movies on a Saturday evening may be all you need to rejuvenate for the week. So what do you need? You could start by buying your favorite products from your local spa after your visit. Or you can take a trip to your local mall or drugstore for remarkably affordable and top-quality home spa items. By far, my favorite skin-care line is Olay Regenerist. The Detoxifying Pore Scrub and the Microdermabrasion and Peel System give instant glow and smoothness that rival the results of any one-hour facial. In fact, the relatively cheap Regenerist line performed slightly better than the expensive brands it was up against in a December 2006 *Consumer Reports* study comparing the efficacy of antiwrinkle creams. And if you love facials like I do, then you appreciate the clean feeling you get from pore extraction. That's why I always have Bioré pore and face strips at home. They are my favorite beauty-care invention because you can literally *see* the results! Aveda has a wonderful Tourmaline Mask that I use while I soak in the tub. My favorite bath and body products are from a company called Deep Sea Cosmetics. Every woman has her personal favorites as well as her unique beauty needs. Test out a few and stock up on your favorites so you can relax and feel pampered any day of the week!

7. The Daily System

I'm a huge fan of Pottery Barn's "Daily System," a kitchen or office organizing system that can be purchased at their online site. I have a wall in my kitchen devoted to this space-saving beauty in white (it also comes in black and espresso stain). Since we've had the system in our home, fewer papers get lost, and it's easier to find pens, paper clips, and measuring tape—you know, all the little things that hold you up in a day. The cool thing is that you can customize the wall system to meet your family's needs. If you hate when papers and supplies pile up on the kitchen table, then you need to get a wall system that keeps you and your family organized!

8. Shout Stain Wipes

Along with tissues and hand sanitizer, no mom's purse should be without individually packaged Shout Stain Wipes. Unlike the stain-remover pens that can leak or even evaporate, Shout Wipes are packaged like those little wipes they give you at restaurants where finger foods are served. From chocolate to cranberry juice, these little wipes will remove any stain in an instant so you and the kids can remain stain-free during outings and prevent stains from setting in before you get home. And they're not just for when you're out with the kids. I once took a wine stain out of my husband's cream turtleneck while we were out alone for dinner, allowing him to enjoy the rest of our night without thinking about a big purple mark on the front of his sweater. He was amazed. It saved our evening—and reminded him of why he can't live without me!

9. Frozen Cookie Dough

I'm the first to admit that I'm not much of a baker. I can do it, but I just don't enjoy the measuring and precision needed for good results. At Christmas and during snow days, I'll bust out the flour and the measuring cups and bake with my kids. The rest of the year, though, I rely on my sister-in-law Brigid's cookies. She's an avid baker and periodically sends a shoe box of cookies that I keep in the freezer. On days that I feel like giving the kids a special treat, I'll take out a few before I leave to pick up the kids from school. By the time I come home, they're defrosted and ready to serve with milk. For my birthday, Brigid always sends me her delicious cookies so I can freeze them and always have some on hand. On cold winter afternoons, however, nothing beats a warm cookie coming out of the oven—or the delicious smell wafting through the house. I also love watching my kids gather around the oven door, turning the interior light on and off, anxiously waiting for me to pull the tray out to their *oohs* and *aahs*. That's why I keep frozen cookie dough in the freezer. I know it's a little more expensive, but it's a small luxury that makes my kids' day and allows a baking-challenged mom like me to feel like the coolest mom in town! My favorite is called Better Bakes from the Immaculate Baking Company in Flat Rock, North Carolina. You can feel good about this mini-extravagance because they are made of all-natural and or-ganic ingredients and the company donates a portion of its pro-ceeds to charitable causes.

10. Yummie Tummie Tanks and T-Shirts

Sure, a lot of people heard about this incredible shaper tank from Oprah, but I had to put it on my list in case you missed it, because so many moms face the problem of creating a smooth silhouette under their clothes. I like their "strappy" tank, and I wear it under almost everything I wear. The fabric and design are comfortable, and the tummy control in the midsection reminds me to straighten up and improve my posture. Yummie Tummie even has a tank just for nursing moms, with a comfortable snap-down bust panel that also smoothes out stubborn post-baby midsections. At eighty dol-lars a pop, these so-soft tanks are not so cheap, but you only need one or two. I say it's worth the splurge! After five babies, I can use all the help I can get!

11. Kitchen Timer

A kitchen timer has a multitude of uses for moms that go well beyond preventing burned cookies. Your timer can be used to keep track of time-outs and help your children conceptualize their pun-ishment. In addition, a buzzer prevents Mom from forgetting about someone being on time-out. That's happened to me several times, and I felt horrible! If you have multiple kids, you'll find that timers help kids take turns better than Mom can because there is real power in the buzzer. If I say, "You can play with it for ten min-utes, and then it's your brother's turn," I may very well still encoun-ter resistance when the time is up. But for some reason the sound of the buzzer makes them just hand it over. A timer will also help your child keep track of their daily reading requirements. Our kids are required to read at least thirty minutes a day, and I get far fewer complaints when I hand them a timer and instructions to read until it goes off. My sister-in-law uses her timer to limit her son's computer habits. Finally, I love to use my timer for cleanup competitions. Kids love to beat the timer! Set it for five or ten minutes, and challenge your kids to pick up their rooms before the timer goes off. You'll be amazed at how quickly they can clean their rooms! If you're a serious cook or if you have more than one child, consider purchasing the Chef's Quad Timer. Among many other cool features, it allows you to keep track of four different times so you can simultaneously bake cookies and a casserole while monitoring your teenager's computer usage and keeping track of your four-year-old's time-out!

12. Smartmomjewelry.com

The designers behind Smartmomjewelry wanted to create jewelry that Mom would love wearing and that could simultaneously soothe and entertain her teething baby—especially the ones who love to tug on our jewelry. They call it Teething Bling. How's that for dual function?! These pendants come in many different colors, including their latest and very fashionable metallic collection. It's so cute you'll love wearing it long after your baby needs a distracting teething activity at a restaurant or in church to keep her quiet. It caught my attention because over the years, I have had several beautiful beaded necklaces yanked off my neck by one of my babies. Eventually, I stopped wearing neck jewelry for fear that my baby might swallow a bead. Smartmom pendants and bangles are made of the highest-quality, phthalate-free, federally approved silicone.

The material is nontoxic, latex free, and food safe, and it can even be washed in the dishwasher! It is the same silicone used in many other popular teething products. Teething Bling pendants make my list because they are an affordable luxury (under fifteen dollars) that can go beyond the teething years and be enjoyed as a cool, funky piece of jewelry anytime.

13. Loungewear

In the beginning, every stay-at-home mom swears she will present herself in public pulled together in style. Eventually, however, we all fall prey to the need for comfort and the reality that much of our day is spent outside of the public eye. It's so easy to get caught up in our kids and some activity and then realize that we have to dress the kids and be out the door in five minutes to pick up the others from school or some other appointment. That's why every mom should have at least two comfortable yet great-looking outfits that can go from home to store or school with style. I have two personal favorites. I love the funky yet comfortable look of the loungewear from Anthropologie.com, and the soft, supercomfy loungewear sold by Barefoot Dreams strikes that perfect balance between casual and pulled together. Unfortunately, Barefoot Dreams' clothes are not sold online. You can, however, go to their Web site and find retailers near you. Beware; they have beautiful baby products too!

14. Jeans You Love

In the casual world of an at-home mom, a pair of jeans you love is an absolute must-have! Since every woman's body is different, I can't recommend a specific brand because all of us have different shapes, but I do insist you invest in one great pair of jeans that is fashionable and that you feel great in. There's no excuse for ill-fitting "mom jeans" because today's jeans have been engineered to flatter any body type and camouflage your flaws. The trick to finding the right pair is to first go online and do some research. Plenty of sites will give you clues based on your height and body shape. Then, go to a department store or boutique that specializes in denim. The store you select should have a wide variety of designer brands so you have a wide array of fits to choose from. Shop for jeans without kids and on a day you have *plenty* of time. Bring along a trusted friend you can count on to be honest. The money and time you spend finding the perfect jeans for your body are time well spent. It is a staple item you should never skimp on!

15. Epicurious.com

I absolutely love this cooking Web site and use it all the time! In many ways, I credit it (along with the Food Network) with teaching me how to cook. For one thing, the site is super-easy to use. And it allows you to search by ingredients, so you can find hundreds of things you can do with only the ingredients you have on hand in your fridge and pantry. Another feature I love is that each recipe is ranked in different categories by a range of zero to four forks. I always look at the recipes' user rankings and comments. If a recipe has four forks on Epicurious, you can be sure it's a winner! This site is trolled by serious at-home cooks who take the time to add suggestions to improve or modify each recipe. If there's a consensus among the comments that you should double the garlic—do it! Finally, another cool feature on the site is that it allows you to store recipes in a file under your name on their site. For a quick and easy gift, Epicurious.com allows you to select recipes from your file and order a hardcover cookbook with your family's favorite dishes for friends and relatives. How's that for a gift with a very personal touch?

16. Sunglasses

Sunglasses are the easiest way to make a fashion statement. By simply keeping up with eyewear trends, you can seem "with it" without having to do a wardrobe overhaul. Another reason time-strapped at-home moms need a great pair of sunglasses is that they hide a multitude of sins. No time for makeup? Puffy, tired eyes from late-night feedings? No problem! With a cool pair of shades, you can drop the kids off at school without feeling like a slug!

17. Sunscreen

Recent studies have proven that sunscreen, as opposed to fancy, expensive antiwrinkle moisturizers, is the number-one protection against signs of aging and wrinkles. It is perhaps the cheapest beauty investment you can make. At-home moms need sunscreen because we spend so much time outdoors at the park, watching games, working out, or walking the dog. Just as important, we spend plenty of time in the car, and the sun's harmful rays come through the car window, which is why, upon careful inspection, many people will find more sun damage on the side of their face that faces the window. Getting into the sunscreen habit, including in the winter months, is an easy and cheap way for at-home moms to stay beautiful! For your face, be sure to select a sunscreen especially for the face so it won't clog your pores and cause breakouts. Or choose a facial moisturizer that contains sunscreen, such as

Bobbi Brown's tinted moisturizer with SPF 15, to cut time off your morning routine.

18. A Night Off Cooking for Mom!— www.cookingfordads.com

About twice a year, usually New Year's Eve and Valentine's Day, Sean buys sushi-grade fish to make homemade sushi for me. We both love sushi, but I think what I love most is that since he enjoys rolling sushi, I don't have to do anything! I sit at the table with a glass of wine and enjoy the experience of watching my husband cook for me. As much as I love cooking, I also like taking a break from it! We don't have a lot of good take-out options in our town, so I used to think, "If only Sean were a better cook, I'd take more days off." Then I discovered the Web site www.cookingfordads.com (Father's Day gift alert: there's also a DVD). The host, Rob Barrett, is a regular dad who provides easy recipes and step-by-step instruction in an entertaining way that even the most kitchen-challenged dads, like Sean, can handle. Rob walks Dad right through the process so everyone can feel good about Mom taking the night off!

19. Candles

Have you ever noticed that women love to gift candles to one another? The reason is that we *love* candles—the smell, the mood they set, and the signals they send to our brains. Scientists know that we can alter our moods through our senses, and the fastest way to do it is through our sense of smell. Whether you keep one on your night table, by your bathtub, or near the cozy window seat where you like to read, a candle is a small luxury that can help Mom relax and transition after a long day with kids. My favorite is by Voluspa in French Bourbon Vanille.

20. A Cozy "Mom Chair"

Remember when Dad had his own "chair" that no one dared sit in? Well, I believe that today's mom should have *her* own comfy upholstered chair, but instead of being off-limits, it should actually be large enough for Mom to curl up in with a good book, a nursing baby, or a couple of kids for a bedtime story. One woman I know keeps her chair in the bathroom so she can read books to her boys while they take a bath—or simply escape to when she needs alone time! If my bathroom were big enough, I'd probably do the same. But since it isn't, I moved my armchair out of my living room and into my kitchen so I'm always part of the action. In the morning I nurse the baby in my chair. In the afternoon it's everyone's favorite story-time location. At night, when the kids go to bed, I make a cup of tea and watch the late-night comics. There are so many beautiful memories created in my chair that I can't imagine living without one. So if you're looking to gift *yourself* something for your baby shower, birthday, or Mother's Day, how about a very comfortable armchair that you can create memories in for years to come?

10

HONOR YOUR LEGACY

Putting Your Choice in Perspective

- Recording Your Legacy

- Journaling Your Family's Stories

- Create Cards and a Family Web Site

- Go Easy on Yourself

- It's Not Just Physical—It's Emotional!

- Loving the Process

$\mathcal{W}$e do not remember days. . . .

We remember moments

—CESARE PAVESE

~~~~~~

As an at-home mom, I have chosen the nurturing of my family as my primary legacy, and it deserves to be appropriately honored! One way I do this is by documenting my work and my family's life together. When my work is laid out in front of me, I can appreciate what I do in a way that is frankly difficult to do in the middle of a typical busy day. Whether it's a photograph, a screen saver, a cleverly designed family Web site, a fun family Christmas card, a journal, or a home movie set to songs that capture this particular moment in my family's life, taking the time to document my family is time well spent. We need to be reminded of our important work so we can appreciate and enjoy it now. Why wait twenty years to savor the memories; savoring them now encourages me to take pleasure in the present. In these captured moments, I can see taking shape a life that is richer for having followed my heart and desire to devote this season of my life to my children and my family. There are so many pleasurable aspects of mothering. I love being a mother. Tapping into the pride I feel for my part in nurturing this family encourages me to keep going, especially on those days that seem hard and long. It encourages me to focus less on the daily struggles and more on the satisfaction I am gaining from a life well lived in the company of those I love most.

Too often, these feelings are dismissed as "sentimental" or "corny." Some might even feel that it is not intellectually respectable for women who have spent a significant number of years accumulating degrees to contemplate the pleasures and satisfactions of mothering. As a result, too many are reluctant to talk about it, much less flaunt it. If they focus on the joys, of which there are many, instead of dwelling on the difficulties, they are said to be "wearing rose-colored glasses." I hear that very often from people who visit my blog! It's as if they refuse to believe that I can truly be happy and fulfilled by what I do. It's so strange to me.

In the work world, we hear all the time about CEOs, small-business owners, professionals, and entrepreneurs who toil very long, hard hours, but still love what they do. Imagine for a second Oprah's day. Sure there's a degree of glamour there, but don't kid yourself—she works grueling hours. But since she's doing what she loves, her focus, and thus ours, is on the positive aspects of her job. When hardworking professionals express their love and passion for what they do, we do not question the joy their work brings to their lives. Talk to an at-home mom who is equally passionate and positive about her job, though, and many people think she is either in denial or, worse, some sort of Stepford wife! Nothing could be further from the truth. If being an at-home parent is truly your desire, as it is mine, then there is nothing wrong with that. Don't apologize and don't question it. And there is nothing suspect or old-fashioned about wanting to dedicate yourself full-time to the care of your children and family. It is certainly within your rights to celebrate your choice and your family—right now, in the present!

Recording Your Legacy

Start with photographs. This is a simple way to remind yourself of your work and how wonderful it is. That's one reason why next to the kitchen sink (a place I often find myself in the course of my day), I keep a visual reminder of what I do and why I do it: a beautiful framed black-and-white photograph of me jostling a then one-year-old Jack on my hip. It is a candid mother-son moment that captures the authentic me. Whereas a mommy motto motivates you, this visual reminder does more: it also celebrates motherhood! That's why even though I'm wearing faded jeans and almost no makeup in that photograph, I find it more beautiful than any of the industry head shots I've taken over the years.

If we want to celebrate our legacy today with visual reminders of our life's work, we have to get the photographs out of that box in the closet and off of the computer. Sure, we e-mail a few to the grandparents. But once we download them, many of us rarely enjoy them again. I have a friend who never opened the photo drawer until she had to—to find pictures for her daughter's high school graduation video. She had always wanted to go through the drawer, but as the years passed, the dread increased, and she kept procrastinating until she could no longer avoid it. After sorting through the pictures with her daughter, however, she told me how much she regretted not doing it sooner. She wasted so much time feeling anxious about it. In fact, it turned out to be an incredible bonding experience and a truly enjoyable activity. "Even though we didn't organize them, it was fun to look at them and select our favorites for the graduation movie." And that's the point: if we approach the photo situation as one giant overwhelming "to-do" project, of course it's going to cause anxiety. Who needs that pressure? Let's look at it as something we do for ourselves, a pleasurable activity in which we simply go through them not to organize, but to remind ourselves of this life we are building. If some organization happens along the way, great! But that's not the purpose.

To honor your legacy doesn't mean you have to organize the drawer or print every picture off the computer. Just select a few photos that capture your vision of motherhood and family and display them. Frames are cheap these days, and nothing personalizes your home and brings more warmth and history to it than photographs. You can even turn a beloved photo into a piece of art: there are Web sites that will enlarge and print your photo onto a canvas of any size. Framed or not, these photos are worthy of being hung in a place of importance in your home.

My own mother always had pictures displayed prominently in our home, but never properly scrapbooked until the nest was empty. By that time, she could hardly remember who was who among the newborn-baby pictures, and as a result, album viewing in our family involves a considerable amount of debate regarding dates and places. It was my own mother's admonition not to leave it for one big empty-nest project that first prompted me to keep my photos in some semblance of order. Though by no stretch perfect, my first rudimentary photo-organization session resulted in a series of photo boxes kept in some degree of chronological order.

Then, a few years ago, on a cold Wisconsin evening, despite my protestations, my friend Melissa coerced me into joining her for a scrapbooking night at a local church hall. I was dubious but she insisted. "Just bring a stack of recent photos of the kids," she told me. I had no idea what this was all about, except I figured she had an outstanding Tupperware or Pampered Chef obligation to settle and my presence was part of the deal. What a revelation! Though I did "scrap" a page that night with a few of the photos from my pile, I spent most of my time at the event looking through everyone else's scrapbooks as they worked. There were so many beautiful books! These mothers had truly created family heirlooms. I could sense their pride as they watched me turn the pages of their books. I realized that the time they spent creating them was soothing and rewarding and that scrapbooks are as much a gift to a family as they are to the person who made them. And so, though I only reluctantly attended, I returned home that night with a genuine desire to write my own family's story—and about one hundred fifty dollars' worth of scrapbooking materials and tools.

I was excited to get started. My first book was dedicated to our family vacation in Spain. Once I dug the photos out of the box, I could journal, write captions, and personalize my book to echo the spirit of our trip. My family loved it! Six years later, when I look at the scrapbook, I am reminded of stories I never would have remembered had I not taken the time to write them down. I know not everyone is "arts and crafty," and you may consider scrapbooking the height of tedium. But if you're the type to enjoy the creative process involved, you will find such joy in seeing your family story unfold before you.

I personally love the process, but it's seeing the final product that gives me the most pleasure because each book is like a love letter to my family and to myself. Thankfully, technology has improved as the size of my family has increased. With five kids, including an infant, I no longer have time for traditional scrapbooking, let alone for making individual books for each child. Since virtually every picture I now take is digital and downloaded onto my computer, I use scrapbooking computer programs. My time-saving trick is to wait till the end of the year for a one-stop scrapbooking experience. During the lazy days between Christmas and New Year's Day, my family goes through the photos from that year. All of the ones we like, we put into a folder on the computer. Then I download them into a digital scrapbook program that allows me to select a scrapbook style, photo sizes, layouts, and captions. (You don't even have to bother with captions or explanations; knowing the year may be enough to jog your memories.) I can make them as elaborate or simple as I like, but I've found that even the most elaborate computer-generated scrapbook is far less time-intensive than the simplest handmade traditional scrapbook. Once it's downloaded, I can order a hardcover personalized photo album for the year. I keep it simple and still enjoy the final product—a family heirloom that honors our family and my work!

Journaling Your Family's Stories

How many times do you swear to write down those funny stories and observations by your kids at the end of the day? Then when the evening comes, you say, "Oh, I could never forget that. I'll write it down tomorrow." By the next day, however, you forgot the *way* your daughter said it, and by the third day, you forgot what was said at all. At a baby shower I received a beautiful journal for writing down these memories. The book was lovely, so lovely that I hated writing in it because I didn't want to make a mistake or write hurriedly in poor handwriting. Because the book was so beautiful, I would only write in the book when I was totally relaxed and in the mood to write leisurely and with much thought. In other words, I rarely ever wrote in the book! Then recently I decided to purchase several cheap spiral notebooks. In a school notebook, I felt less worried about being neat or eloquent. In fact, I could instruct my seven- or nine-year-old to "Go write that story down for me" while I filled the dishwasher or chopped vegetables for dinner. Besides, there's a bonus in having others, especially children, write the story. Thirty years from now, we'll all appreciate those backward letters and misspelled words.

I have discovered it's important to have several notebooks or journals around the house, as opposed to just one in the night table drawer. That way, you can always have one nearby, when you're in the moment. You'll never get all those cute things written down, but if having several in various areas of the house encourages you to write down even a few of them, it's well worth the dollar ninety-nine you paid for them!

Create Cards and a Family Web Site

At Christmas time, I spend a great deal of thought and time on the family Christmas card. I search for the best photos of the year and spend hours on the layout, the greeting, and even the theme. Usually, our card also includes a custom drawing from our family's resident artist, my daughter Evita. Last year, our theme was lumberjacks. On the card are pictures of the kids in the lumberjack pajamas we bought them for Christmas, a photo of Sean when he chopped down the Christmas tree, and a family shot in front of a woodpile outside of our home. Hokey? You betcha—as they say in Wisconsin! But for me the card is not just a holiday greeting to friends and relatives. It's a gift to myself: a reminder of where so much of my energy and time has gone this year—my family. And frankly, I feel good about it. Every time I put the year's card into the photo album where I keep a copy of every year's Christmas card, I can't help looking back on the years—and the beautiful cards— with pride.

And when it comes to the Christmas cards, I give myself another gift: the gift of time. I never, ever pressure myself to mail them out before Christmas when holiday preparations are at an all-time high. My deadline is to get them out before Valentine's Day, though this year, on account of the book, they were accompanied by an Easter family letter on pink stationery! I've just decided to feel good about knowing that we are the last ones to wish our friends and relatives holiday greetings.

A family Web site is another excellent way to honor and share your legacy—and an easy way for grandparents to get the latest updates and photos of the grandkids. In my family, Sean and the kids run the Web site, and they regularly upload pictures, home movies, scanned artwork (storing kids' artwork digitally is a big space saver!), school awards, and anything else of meaning and importance to our family. These are important times for you and your family, and finding ways to reflect on them now, in the present, gives you an opportunity to appreciate what you are building now, not years from now! When our parents and older friends tell us that time flies, we know they are right. The question then becomes, how can I slow it down? You can't! But you can consciously find ways to appreciate its fragility and fleetingness in the present, before it is long gone.

Go Easy on Yourself

When it comes to honoring your choice to be an at-home parent, the best advice I can give is to be easy on yourself! Being an at-home mom is a big job, and it's OK if you don't always love it or if you have days when you can't wait until Dad gets home to take over. It certainly doesn't mean that you are a bad mom or that you made a bad choice in choosing to be home caring for your kids. It just means you're having a hard day—and in any job there are bound to be good and bad days.

Recognizing that full-time parenting has its own unique challenges is one of the most important things every at-home mom must do. Unlike with other jobs, being in the company of children means days filled with many little interruptions—tying a shoe, dressing a doll, finding the screwdriver to put new batteries in a toy, and cleaning up spills. It can be difficult to start, let alone finish, projects, and that's why so many moms feel unproductive or even downright hopeless at the end of some days. But the act of nurturing and caring for children was never intended to be measured by the standards of productivity used in professions outside of the home because much of what you do is unquantifiable. It is impossible to quantitatively measure the value of a hug, a well-deserved time-out, or the security your children are gaining from spending their day in the company of their mommy. Frankly, it's about time we as mothers begin to respect our "nurturing"; when we do, we are taking an important step toward changing our culture's consciousness. Presently, our culture places higher value on our society's "producers," and this has had significant consequences for children.

One of the hardest parts about being in the trenches of child-rearing—especially with young children—is that it can be very difficult to measure your progress and achievements. There's no sales quota to meet at the end of the quarter, or profits to tally and compare at the end of the month or year. This has always been a serious challenge for me. By nature, I thrive on several things that are difficult, if not impossible on many days, to achieve as an at-home mom: organization, feeling productive, a sense of accomplishment, and of course affirmation. I have learned to handle this struggle by recognizing progress in other ways, concentrating on those things I can change or improve (like my children's behavior or skills), and not allowing myself to become demoralized by the things I can't change (like a disorganized house when my baby is teething and just wants to be held all day). This acceptance is perhaps the greatest lesson I have learned as a mom. It's also one I have to periodically RELEARN!

First, be honest and ask yourself if you could be more productive or organized. Are you using your time wisely? The answer should come only from within, not by comparing yourself to anyone else. Ask yourself how you feel about the use of your time, your daily schedule, and your environment. Some things are within your control; others are not. I happen to be in a better mood and think more clearly when my house is organized and somewhat tidy. I also know that I have some degree of control over it. Since it is a priority for me, I carve out time in my day to keep my house clean and organized; I invest time in teaching and training my kids to help with chores; and I have adjusted my budget to allow for some hired help so I can get it done and move on to more enjoyable activities. Some days, I will not be able to attain the level of order I prefer, but the important thing is that I have recognized this need and the degree of control I have over it.

Just don't adopt someone else's priorities as your own. If your house is messy but it doesn't bother you, great! Who cares what other people do? If you have better things to do, then your goal should be to learn to live with the mess. Seriously! Don't waste time and energy beating yourself up over it. If you can be a better mom by letting go of the small stuff, or living with a messier house, then by all means do it! If, on the other hand, the messy drawers in your kids' rooms drive you nuts every time you open them, then make time to clean them out so you can get on with enjoying your day and your kids! The truth is that at-home moms accomplish so many important things every day—things that cannot be quantified or presented at the end of the day as proof of accomplishment. Intuitively, you know that the personal and intimate work of motherhood is intangible. At the end of the day, no one will know exactly what you did, much less the love and care you put into those actions. Accept that fact and give yourself the love and appreciation you deserve.

It's Not Just Physical—It's Emotional!

Parenting is an emotional task, and while all parents are called to meet their child's emotional and developmental needs, the at-home parent does this many more hours in a day! This can be as taxing as any of the physical demands of parenting. For one thing, an at-home mom is role-modeling and teaching virtually all day, and we know our children are watching! Make one slipup on the phone call with my sister and it's "Mom, you said a bad word!" Recently, my four-year-old admonished me for not really paying attention to her when she was talking. She put her hands around my face, turned my head toward hers, and with her face right in front of mine, declared, "You're not listening! You're 'posed to listen to your chil'ren."

Discipline is always an emotional topic for parents, but perhaps more so for stay-at-home moms, who are on the front lines all day long. Good parents know that it takes much more effort to discipline lovingly than harshly. Putting a child on a series of time-outs rather than yelling or spanking takes more time. So does talking with your child afterward about how families should treat one another and a little more time spent after that hugging and tickling so that they know that everything is fine. It can take extraordinary effort to resist losing your temper when your toddler dumps out his dresser drawers for the seventh time, or to forgive yourself when you do. These are the things that make at-home motherhood the complicated, messy, beautiful job that it is. At-home parenting can also be emotionally draining because we feel that the stakes are so high. Like all parents, we have so much invested in our children and want so badly to do a great job. But having made the choice to do this full-time, we often have higher expectations of ourselves and can be very, very critical of ourselves. Don't fall into that trap. Accept the emotional component (and your human imperfections) as part of the job.

Loving the Process

Being an at-home parent does not make you a better parent. What it does afford you is more opportunities to become the best parent you can be. Like any activity or sport you love, the more time you spend doing it, the more skills you acquire. At some point, the skills and techniques get easier, almost second nature. More important, becoming a better player often translates into many more opportunities to truly enjoy the game—or in this case, delight in our children.

Of course, the more we desire to be the best parents we can be, the more disappointing it can be when we experience setbacks or failures. However, no one is perfect, and no matter how much you love your child, he or she is bound to test your nerves. When we lose our patience with our kids, it's important to seek their forgiveness and model the art of an apology. In our family, we have the "do over" to encourage the concept that everybody gets a second chance. When they are very little, we explain the concept of a "do over" and practice it with them. A "do over" means putting the child outside of the room they are currently misbehaving in, closing the door, and asking them to knock when they are ready for their "do over." When they come around to knocking, we say, "Oh, is the nice Lucia knocking?" From behind the door, they sheepishly say yes and slowly open the door. As soon as we see their little face, we shout, "Welcome back!" and shower them with hugs and kisses. Then it's all over. Now our older kids know that a simple offer of a "do over" gives them a no-questions-asked opportunity to start fresh. Thankfully, it works both ways (though the little ones expect that we go through the process of knocking), and our kids have learned to give us the same kind of forgiveness. We need it.

In the end, though, it can be far more difficult to forgive ourselves. But we must. We are not born good parents. We learn to be good parents. Certainly a desire to read and learn about child psychology and child development is helpful for any parent. Books about the Montessori method, the emotional life of toddlers, the spiritual potential of children, and various theories and techniques on disciplining line my bookshelves. But they can only do so much. Ultimately, intuition and good old trial and error are the primary tools of parenting. The good news about at-home parenting is that the more time you spend in the company of your child, the more opportunities you have to understand your child, meet his unique psychological and developmental needs, and get on with the business of delighting in him! For the at-home parent, there will be more opportunities to fall short of our own expectations because there are so many more opportunities for interaction. But that also means that there are more occasions to reconcile and plenty of time to learn about and from one another in the process. This is the work of at-home motherhood, and valuing it permits us to find joy and meaning in even our bad days. After all, we are not seeking perfection in our life and relationships, but rather authenticity. Who better than children to remind us of the merit of authenticity?

Sean and I have often talked about feeling lucky to have had our children in our late twenties and thirties, when we were old enough to grasp the fleeting nature of the child-rearing years. We know it is moving quickly and more so due to the number of children we have. And yet, even in the fatigue and chaos that is a house and life with five children under the age of ten, we already sense the nostalgia and yearning we will feel for this time in our lives. This awareness has a way of coloring our interactions, softening our edges and helping us hold on to the moments for just little bit longer. It is an indescribable gift and blessing in our life.

Thankfully, there does come a time when a mother begins to see the fruits of her labor. It reveals itself in small ways and often catches us by surprise. You overhear your children speaking politely and intelligently with another adult. Your five-year-old masters his knife and fork skills—something you have been spending time teaching him. You witness your toddler in a moment of deep empathy for his sibling, kissing and hugging her after she falls. These are moments that remind us that what we do matters because we know that our child would be less likely to have developed this skill without our daily presence. This is certainly not meant to diminish our child's accomplishment or detract from his individuality, but rather to affirm what we know to be true—that we are our child's first and best teacher.

The ideas and techniques for enjoying at-home motherhood that I have shared in this book are ideas that have worked for me. These principles aren't complicated. The secret, however, is that every at-home mom, including this one, has to periodically be reminded of them. At-home moms are particularly susceptible to the error of depleting one's self in an effort to care for others. We must recommit, sometimes daily (even hourly!), to replenishing and taking excellent care of ourselves—because our task is very important and sometimes difficult, and requires us to be in our best physical and mental shape. Like most moms, at-home moms are guilty of underestimating or downplaying our contributions. However, we have chosen an extraordinary vocation, and we should celebrate the gift that is motherhood. So often, advice and guides for at-home moms are pitched to help moms "survive," the implication being that survival is the goal. I couldn't disagree more! I don't want to *survive*. I want to *thrive* and enjoy this journey in a joyful and optimistic state.

The state of at-home motherhood has changed dramatically, and so have the women choosing it. Today's at-home mom is bringing more education and life experience to the job than any other generation before her. The decision to be an at-home mom is a powerful one made out of love that will have lasting benefits for your family and your children. These are honorable outcomes. But equally important is the woman, the mother herself. My hope is that my book will remind at-home moms to recognize and even indulge in the many pleasurable aspects of our work and to bask in the satisfaction that can be derived from doing it well. Taking care of ourselves so we feel refreshed and energized, eliminating guilt, and finding creative short cuts so we have more time to know, engage, and revel in our children should be the goal of every at-home mom, and it is the primary purpose of this book. This is a fruitful and exciting season of your life. Your decision to stay home and enjoy it to its fullest so you and your children can look back on this time with warmth and wonder is a powerful one. Truly internalizing this simple and profound truth is our daily mission. That is the secret to staying home and staying happy.

Television host, pundit, and mother of five **Rachel Campos-Duffy** is well-known for discussing the hot topics of the day in her signature honest, articulate, and down-to-earth style on national media outlets like CNN, CNN.com, MSNBC, and FOX.

Rachel started her television career as a pioneer of reality TV on MTV's groundbreaking reality show *The Real World, San Francisco* and went on to make numerous guest-hosting appearances on *The View*. Along with Florence Henderson, she cohosted *Speaking of Women's Health* on the Lifetime Network.

She frequently appears on national talk shows and is a parenting expert for AOL, where she writes a weekly column for Parentdish.com. She also contributes to Anderson Cooper's CNN 360 blog, as well as the Catholic News Agency and other Catholic online and radio programming.